On Appreciating Congress

ON POLITICS

L. Sandy Maisel, Series Editor

On Politics is a new series of short reflections by major scholars on key subfields within political science. Books in the series are personal and practical as well as informed by years of scholarship and deliberation. General readers who want a considered overview of a field as well as students who need a launching platform for new research will find these books a good place to start. Designed for personal libraries as well as student backpacks, these smart books are small format, easy reading, aesthetically pleasing, and affordable.

Books in the Series

LOUIS FISHER

ON APPRECIATING
CONGRESS
The People's Branch

Paradigm Publishers
Boulder • London

To Mickey Edwards and David Skaggs

Copyright © 2010 Paradigm Publishers

Published in the United States by Paradigm Publishers, 3360 Mitchell Lane, Suite E, Boulder, CO 80301 USA.

Paradigm Publishers is the trade name of Birkenkamp & Company, LLC, Dean Birkenkamp, President and Publisher.

Library of Congress Cataloging-in-Publication Data

Fisher, Louis.
　On appreciating Congress / Louis Fisher.
　　　p. cm. — (On politics)
　Includes bibliographical references and index.
　ISBN 978-1-59451-794-5 (hardcover : alk paper)
　ISBN 978-1-59451-795-2 (paperback : alk paper)
1.　United States. Congress. 2.　Legislative power—United States. 3. Separation of powers—United States. I. Title.
　JK1041.F57 2009
　328.73—dc22

　　　　　　　　　　　　　　　　　2009027138

Printed and bound in the United States of America on acid-free paper that meets the standards of the American National Standard for Permanence of Paper for Printed Library Materials.

Designed and Typeset by Cheryl Hoffman.

14 13 12 11 10　　　　1 2 3 4 5

CONTENTS

PREFACE

This book explains why Congress is the indispensable institution for safeguarding popular, democratic, and constitutional government. No doubt its record over the past two centuries presents a mixed picture, with many plusses and minuses. Having worked for Congress for the past four decades, I am well aware of its shortcomings. The records of the other two branches are also decidedly mixed, and yet they escape much of the public wrath. Portraying Congress as so inherently inept that it must be kept subordinate to presidential and judicial power is misguided and uninformed.

The virtues widely attributed to the president and the Supreme Court are greatly exaggerated. This book spells out why. Second, the framers looked to Congress as the first branch because it is the institution through which citizens at the local and state levels engage in self-government. Although presidents claim to be the "national representative," they cannot substitute for the knowledge and legitimacy brought by members of Congress. Third, weaken or downgrade Congress and you undercut the hope and future of democracy. The eventual result: a system where citizens vote for lawmakers but the important decisions of public policy are left primarily to nonelected executive officials and federal judges. In other words, citizens are asked to return to their lowly category as "subjects."

Chapter 1 traces the slow and uneven growth of democracy. After much bloodshed, citizens gained the right to exercise control over their lives by voting for public officials to represent and protect their interests. Democratic government affirms the worth and dignity of individuals by recognizing their right to participate in public policy, not only during elections but throughout the year. In tension with this model at all times is the persistent belief that monarchs, aristocrats, and experts are the natural and superior wielders of power.

Chapter 2 explores the sources and limits of presidential power, beginning with powers expressly stated in the Constitution and reasonably implied in those powers. From those core powers are added, over the years, other prerogatives variously called emergency, inherent, and residual, converting the president into a political force never imagined by the framers and an ever-present threat to democratic government. Although Americans broke with the British model of monarchy, claims have been made over the years that the U.S. president incorporates many of the powers formerly vested in the British king. Those models undermine republican government and congressional power. The idolatry of the presidency, so popular after World War II, is being challenged today by some scholars, both liberal and conservative.

Chapter 3 examines the role of Congress in shaping and deciding constitutional issues. Unfortunately, it is commonplace today to accept the Supreme Court as the final word on the meaning of the Constitution. Even worse, many members of Congress increasingly take the view that they have no say, and should have no say, on constitutional interpretation. That was never the framers' expectation and was not even the position of Chief Justice John Marshall when he wrote *Marbury v. Madison* (1803). Congress and the president have at various times functioned as coequal (if not superior) interpreters of the Constitution. Genuflection to the judiciary is no less damaging to republican government than obeisance to presidents and their aides. Many pivotal decisions about constitutional values occur outside all three branches of government, giving life to republican principles.

Another common belief is that Congress cannot possibly protect the rights of minorities because it operates by majority vote. For that reason, safeguarding minority rights must be left to the judiciary. That position might seem logical, even unassailable, but Chapter 4 offers repeated examples of Congress protecting the rights of women, blacks, religious minorities, and other groups far better than the courts. Throughout its history, the Supreme Court spent most of its time protecting government or private corporations. Whatever relief it has brought to individuals and minorities is very much a modern development.

Chapter 5 focuses on the weaknesses of Congress, and there are many. Particularly troublesome since World War II is the failure of Congress to protect its core powers over war and spending. Not only has it been unwilling or unable to fight off encroachments from other branches, at times it takes the initiative to surrender its powers to the president and the courts. When it acts in this manner, it weakens its institutional powers and undermines its capacity to protect constituents in congressional districts and the states. Members of Congress take an oath to support and defend the Constitution, not presidents or the Supreme Court.

A concluding chapter, Chapter 6, offers suggestions on what members of Congress might do if they want to function as part of a coequal branch. For a variety of reasons, lawmakers are unlikely to take those steps on their own. Invigorating democracy depends on the willingness of constituents, scholars, the media, and other parts of society to insist that Congress protect itself and check the other branches. Our liberties depend on a confident and independent Congress. As noted in a recent work, the "path to a healthy democracy, in the American context, leads through a robust Congress." Unfortunately, political leaders and news commentators in their critiques of Congress "rarely take stock of Congress as an institution of democracy. Regrettably, neither do scholars."[1] In a separate study, Julian Zelizer describes Congress as "the heart and soul of democracy, the arena where politicians and citizens most directly interact over pressing concerns."[2] This book is written in that spirit.

I began to think about this book after sitting down with political scientist Sandy Maisel and Paradigm vice president Jennifer Knerr. Congress regularly takes a pounding from all sides. I wanted to do a fair treatment, acknowledging the serious problems of the legislative branch but also calling attention to its contributions and its vital role in protecting democracy. Sandy and Jennifer offered many constructive comments at each stage of the project. My thanks to Lauren Arnest for her careful and thoughtful editing.

Reb Brownell, an attorney and congressional staffer, shares my interest in institutional and constitutional issues. His review of the manuscript offered many thoughtful suggestions on how to clarify and deepen the principal themes. My brother, Lee, read the full manuscript and gave me the benefit of a citizen who follows government and is greatly disappointed with what he sees. It was healthy for me to keep in mind his harsh appraisal of Congress. After I finished the manuscript I received from *Boston University Law Review* its symposium issue of April 2009 entitled "The Most Disparaged Branch: The Role of Congress in the Twenty-First Century." I had long ago realized that writing anything complimentary about Congress is an uphill climb.

Friends and colleagues read portions of the manuscript. I sought advice from House and Senate staffers, Democrats and Republicans, current staff and retirees. For congressional staff let me thank Jeff Biggs, Bill Ellis, David Lachmann, Daniel McAdams, Bob Schiff, and Don Wolfensberger. For my valued colleagues at the Library of Congress, my thanks to Rick Beth, Clint Brass, Henry Hogue, Kevin Kosar, Walter Oleszek, Harold Relyea, Mort Rosenberg, and Stephen Stathis. For friends in the academic community, appreciation goes to Dave Adler, Dick Pious, Chris Pyle, Mark Rozell, Mitch Sollenberger, Bob Spitzer, and Charles Tiefer for their comments.

With great pleasure I dedicate the book to Mickey Edwards and David Skaggs. Edwards served for many years as a Republican member of the U.S. House of Representatives from Oklahoma, rising in the party leadership. Skaggs served for years as a Democratic member of the House from Colorado, assigned to such committees as Appropriations and Intelligence. I admired both for the way they defended constitutional values (especially structural checks) and protected the powers of Congress. They were institutionalists then and institutionalists now. After leaving Congress they continue to be active in public service, including with the Constitution Project, where it is my delight to work with them. The country depends on such individuals with their steady, informed, and articulate commitment to a constitutional republic.

—Louis Fisher

CHAPTER ONE
POPULAR GOVERNMENT

Sovereignty was long associated exclusively with royal power. Only in recent centuries has it come to mean government by the people. The U.S. Constitution begins with three powerful words that astonished previous rulers and all of Europe: "We the People." For most of recorded history, men and women accepted that political decisions about their lives were assigned to a select few, either a monarch assisted by courtiers or an aristocracy. The general public was considered too ignorant, incompetent, and socially inferior to participate in public affairs. Like children, they were expected to submit to the direction and control of those who knew best.

Divine Right

To shore up the political power and legitimacy of a monarchy, kings claimed to rule by divine right. No earthly force or authority could constrain the king. Policies and decisions descended from Heaven, even when the results for the country were calamitous. An associated principle held that the king could do no wrong, and therefore no action at law could ever be brought against him. England discovered ways to allow legitimate grievances to be settled by lesser officials.[1] Countries found it convenient to recognize the divine right of the king to offset the same claim of divine right by the pope.[2] The crown represented the headdress or cap of sovereignty. In some political systems the monarch was above the community, but the law was above the monarch.[3]

It would take centuries of political struggle for the system of monarchy and divine right to give way to elected representatives serving in an assembly to protect the general public and check executive power. In Great Britain, Parliament emerged as a separate institution to challenge royal power. The growth of self-government in England led to costly and bloody civil wars, eventually reducing the monarch to a figurehead without political power. The appeal of popular government in the American colonies prompted the Continental Congress to meet in 1774. With the Declaration of Independence two years later, Americans were determined to cast off monarchy and embrace broad public participation.

Monarchy on the Defensive

Royal government in England faced repeated challenges. With the Magna Carta of 1215, King John at Runnymede promised not to capture or imprison a freeman "except by the lawful judgment of his peers or by the law of the land." Royal power now had a secular competitor, at least for the upper class. They were entitled to a legal process that assured fair and public trials. The Magna Carta, marking a concession to barons, was reissued several times by subsequent kings, serving as an initial check on arbitrary and unjust rule. In later years, English kings were often successful in placing the Crown and personal interests above the law and the interests of the country.

Another curb on royal power took the form of the Petition of Right in 1628. Members of the House of Commons drafted language to place limits on arbitrary arrest, imprisonment without cause, forced loans by the king, and martial law. Charles I struggled with financial burdens after embarking on wars against both France and Spain. One remedy was forced loans. Anyone who protested and refused to lend money to the government could face imprisonment. Upon examining draft language of the petition, Charles I offered to grant certain benefits by divine grace. That did not sit well with Parliament. It insisted that new privileges be grounded not in royal grace but as a matter of right.[4]

The existence of natural rights was no more grounded in fact and evidence than the divine right of kings. Each rested on an assumption, a premise, an ideal system. Each claimed to operate on first principles. Over time, in Anglo-American society, individual rights took hold: the right of conscience, the right to hold political and religious opinions without fear of persecution, the right to participate in government. The Declaration of Independence in 1776 would claim: "We hold these truths to be self-evident, that all men are created equal, that they are endowed by their Creator with certain unalienable Rights." Carl Becker observed that the eighteenth century "deified Nature and denatured God."[5]

After Parliament passed the Petition of Right, Charles I decided to rule the country without Parliament and did so from 1629 to 1640. Parliament returned to pass the Triennial Act, requiring the legislative branch to sit every three years whether the king called lawmakers or not. Conflicts between the royalists and Parliament grew worse, leading to years of civil war between the two sides. Charles I was captured and later beheaded, in 1649. During that period, opponents of royal power looked for ways to strengthen popular sovereignty by having Parliament meet on a regular basis and enlarge the right of suffrage.

Ever so slowly, popular rule began to displace monarchical edicts.[6] When Oliver Cromwell took power after Charles I, his military dictatorship and replacement of a king snapped the pretense of divine right. England restored the monarchy with Charles II, followed by James II. As part of the "Bloodless Revolution," James II was expelled and replaced in 1688 by Princess Mary and her husband, William of Orange. Their rule marked another decisive break with divine right. John Locke wrote *Two Treatises of Government* (1690) in part to reject the doctrine of absolute monarchy and divine right. However, once ideas and concepts come on the scene, they rarely disappear entirely. The divine right of kings would later assume new forms of authority called "executive prerogative" and "inherent" presidential power, examined in the next chapter.

Colonial America

Those who settled in American colonies in the 1600s functioned under the jurisdiction and control of British kings and the Parliament. The notion of a monarch governing by divine right was far too abstract for the hardy souls who arrived on the eastern seaboard to eke out an existence under harsh conditions. Survival depended on individual effort, not heavenly assistance or guidance. London, trying to govern the colonies from 3,000 miles away, inevitably exercised less control than it could at home. Popular sovereignty in America took root more than it did in England.

To sustain themselves in the new wilderness, settlers drafted and agreed to abide by social contracts and compacts. Through initiative and adaptation they learned how to build effective government and manage their affairs. Representative assemblies in the colonies met to pass laws more informed and constructive than the broad orders adopted in England could ever assure. Colonists participating in these assemblies produced public policies more acceptable and easier to enforce. Under the press of daily demands, representative assemblies emerged in the colonies to safeguard the people.

Popular consent and a spirit of independence were less political theory than a practical demand. Colonies continued to operate under the king's grant, but royal control was distant and tenuous. To settle problems within their communities, Americans learned skills by meeting in town halls to debate and decide social and political issues. They mastered parliamentary rules and took conscious and sometimes unconscious steps toward self-government. In discovering how to govern themselves and find solutions, they developed confidence, personal integrity, and responsibility.

British difficulty in controlling the colonies was highlighted by the Stamp Act crisis. The exertion of royal power triggered popular resentment and resistance. The French and Indian War, lasting from 1754 to 1763, prompted military operations from the Ohio Valley to Canada and placed great financial burdens on Great Britain. It seemed reasonable to ask Americans to help pay the cost. After England and France signed a peace treaty, the British Parliament passed the Sugar Act, adding a three-penny tax on molasses. The statute proved difficult to administer and enforce, in part because colonists objected to being taxed from London and learned ingenious methods of evasion. In frustration, Parliament searched for other ways to attract much needed revenue.

England turned to the Stamp Act of 1765, placing an excise tax on all documents and articles made of paper. Swept within this statute were such items as court documents, college diplomas, mortgages, pamphlets, newspapers, and even playing cards. Those documents and others had to be printed on paper carrying a stamp embossed by the Treasury Office. Taxes were imposed in varying amounts. How should the statute be administered? From distant London? Parliament decided to ask colonists to enforce the law. Once again there would be taxation without consent.

Americans sent petitions to London to detail their opposition. Resolutions at home declared that colonists were entitled to all the liberties and privileges of people living in England. Constitutional principles, argued these resolutions, required that taxation be decided by representatives chosen by the people. Only in that manner would representatives know "what

Taxes the People are able to bear, or the easiest Method of raising them, and must themselves be affected by every Tax laid on the People."[7]

These initial verbal protests were followed by action. In Boston, an organization later called the Sons of Liberty decided on concrete steps. Initially they hung in effigy the figure of Andrew Oliver, who had been appointed distributor of stamps for Massachusetts. A mob leveled the building he planned to use to distribute the stamps, beheaded his effigy, and threw stones through the windows of his home. The rest of the effigy disappeared in a bonfire. The mob returned to break into his house and wreck furniture and other possessions. By that time Oliver had fled. Although he had yet to receive his commission from London, he promised a group of visitors he would do nothing to carry out the Stamp Act. When the commission arrived, Oliver, under great public pressure, read his resignation.

Whoever seemed willing to enforce the statute in Massachusetts had their homes attacked, including Lieutenant-Governor Thomas Hutchinson. After the instigator of the violence was seized and faced prosecution, a threat by his supporters to destroy the custom-house provided sufficient cause to release him and drop all charges. Later, the stamped papers arrived from London to permit enforcement, but Governor Francis Barnard publicly announced that the papers would not be distributed. On the day the statute formally took effect, November 1, 1765, the courts and other institutions agreed to meet and function without stamps. If courts were crippled because of a lack of stamped paper, creditors and other litigants would be unable to litigate their interests.

Opposition to the Stamp Act spread to other colonies. Warned that a mob would destroy his house, the distributor of stamps in Rhode Island publicly resigned. The distributor in Maryland refused to resign, but after his house was pulled down he had to flee for his life. He later gave up his post, as did distributors in New Hampshire, North Carolina, and Virginia. Individuals in Connecticut, Delaware, and Pennsylvania appointed to implement the statute agreed not to. The distributor for Georgia pledged to enforce the law until his safety was so threatened that within two weeks he left the area. Colonial activities proceeded with unstamped paper. In areas where England closed ports to force compliance with the statute, the economic interests of both colonial and English merchants suffered.

Members of Parliament were deeply offended by mob opposition to law. They debated sending British troops to compel compliance, forcing the Sons of Liberty in various states to prepare for armed resistance. The Stamp Act served to unite Americans around a common cause of shared interests and loyalty, years before the decision to break with England. London merchants pressured Parliament to repeal the statute, which it finally did in February 1766. Americans had tasted freedom from British rule and dominance. Just as they had begun to deny the power of Parliament, they "were beginning to take stronger ground against the authority of the royal prerogative."[8] A small colony confronted a great power and watched England stand down.

Bloodshed would come soon with Lexington and Concord and the War of Independence, yet the Stamp Act helped discredit many American political leaders who supported continuation of British rule. At the same time it elevated the political careers of those willing to fight for independence, individual freedom, self-government, and the repudiation of monarchy. Service in the French and Indian War from 1754 to 1763 gave military experience to many Americans, including George Washington.

Making the Break

On January 10, 1776, Thomas Paine published *Common Sense*, justifying independence from England. He leveled contempt at the existing process of Americans carrying their grievances to London: "To be always running three or four thousand miles with a tale or a petition, waiting four or five months for an answer, which, when obtained, requires five or six more to explain it in, will in a few years be looked upon as folly and childishness. There was a time when it was proper, and there is a proper time for it to cease." He urged Americans to send delegates from each colony to form a congress for the purpose of deliberating and making law. By rejecting monarchy, in America "*the law is king*. For as in absolute governments the king is law, so in free countries the law *ought* to be king; and there ought to be no other."[9]

Paine explained that monarchies were regularly involved in wars outside the country and civil wars inside. In contrast, republican forms of government in Switzerland and Holland were largely spared military conflicts. Many of the framers reached the same conclusion. When the *Federalist Papers* were published in 1788 to promote ratification of the Constitution, John Jay in Federalist No. 4 warned about the pattern of monarchs and single executives taking their countries into costly and painful wars. Absolute monarchs "will often make war when their nations are to get nothing by it, but for purposes and objects merely personal, such as a thirst for military glory, revenge for personal affronts, ambition, or private compacts to aggrandize or support their particular families or partisans." Executive leaders often engaged in wars "not sanctified by justice or the voice and interests of his people."

To prepare for independence from England, America created the Continental Congress in 1774. Delegates from the colonies met at Philadelphia to protest recent actions by Parliament and petition for a redress of grievances. War began with the battles of Lexington and Concord in April 1775, and two months later Congress created the Continental Army and issued the Declaration of Independence in July 1776. Congress also drafted the Articles of Confederation to define the powers of the new national government.

Throughout this period, there was only one branch of government: the Continental Congress. There was a president of Congress, but he functioned merely as a presiding officer of the legislature, lacking any executive power. There was no separate judiciary. The delegates at the Congress sat on committees to handle administrative questions and judicial disputes. In November 1777, Congress experimented with a board of three commissioners to execute the business of the navy, subject to the direction of the Marine Committee. Congress found the system of boards frustrating because work was too slow and no single officer could be held responsible. The next step came in 1781: the creation of single executives to handle the positions of superintendent of finance, the secretary at war, and the secretary of marine. In that same year, Congress created the office of attorney general to prosecute all suits on behalf of the Confederation of States and to advise Congress on all legal matters submitted to him. These executive officers were purely agents of Congress. They had no independent or separate status.

Much has been written about the framers' dependence on political theories borrowed from foreign writers, such as Montesquieu. What we see in this period with the Continental Congress is less theory and more practice. Year by year the delegates learned which systems of government worked and which did not. Executive and judicial powers originally placed in Congress were spun out with limited autonomy at first and greater discretion later. Congress also established a Court of Appeals in Cases of Capture. The historian Francis Wharton put it very well: The Constitution of 1787 "did not make this distribution of power. It would be more proper to say that this distribution of power made the Constitution of the United States."[10]

Drafting the Constitution

When delegates met at the Philadelphia Convention in 1787, they agreed that the new national government would consist of three separate branches. How separate no one was prepared to say. The Virginia Plan presented on May 29 provided for three branches but made no reference to "separate and distinct" or any other formulation of the separation doctrine. In fact, Congress was to choose the president, and members of Congress were to be joined with the judiciary to form a council of revision, charged with reviewing the constitutionality of legislation. Those ideas did not survive.

Late in July, the Convention adopted a resolution affirming the separation doctrine. The three branches were to be kept distinct and independent, except in specified cases. The version presented on August 6 by the Committee on Detail made no mention of the separation clause and the Constitution was adopted in September and ratified the next year without specific reference to the separation doctrine. The relationships between the branches would have to be worked out in practice. There should be no doubt that the framers rejected the British model that placed all of external affairs, foreign policy, and the war power with the executive. As explained in Chapter 2, not a single one of those powers was granted to the president. They were vested entirely in Congress or shared between the president and the Senate.

In the *Federalist Papers*, James Madison defended the overlapping of powers found in the Constitution. He was a fine writer and political analyst, but in Federalist No. 37 he confessed that words often failed. Just as naturalists had difficulty in defining the precise line between vegetable life and the animal world, so was it impossible to draw the boundary between the three branches of government or "even the privileges and powers of the different legislative branches. Questions daily occur in the course of practice, which prove the obscurity which reigns in these subjects, and which puzzle the greatest adepts in political science."

Much of Madison's analysis of the separation doctrine appears in Federalist No. 47. He acknowledged that tyranny results whenever three branches are concentrated in the same hands, but cautioned that the maxim had been "totally misconceived and misapplied," especially by those who insisted that the three branches had to be totally separate. Montesquieu, he said, could not have intended such separation. In England, the executive magistrate formed a part of the legislative power by making treaties. It shared part of the judicial power by appointing judges. One chamber of Parliament formed a constitutional council for the executive, possessed judicial power in the impeachment process, and exercised supreme appellate jurisdiction in all other cases.

At the state level, Madison could find no instance in which the departments of power had been kept absolutely separate and distinct. What Montesquieu intended, he said, could be no more than this: "that where the *whole* power of one department is exercised by the same hands which possess the *whole* power of another department, the fundamental principles of a free constitution are subverted." During the period when Madison wrote, the strict theory of separation of powers had been replaced by the more practical system of checks and balances. One contemporary pamphleteer referred to the separation doctrine as a "hackneyed principle" and a "trite maxim."[11]

Critics of the draft Constitution attacked the impeachment process because it combined legislative and judicial powers in the same department (the Senate). In Federalist No. 66, Alexander Hamilton dismissed this objection by pointing out that the true meaning of the separation maxim was "entirely compatible with a partial intermixture" and that overlapping was not only "proper, but necessary to the mutual defence of the several members of the government, against each other." To those who complained that the treaty process mixed the president with the Senate, he could only respond wearily in Federalist No. 75 to "the trite topic of the intermixture of powers."

Three states (North Carolina, Pennsylvania, and Virginia) insisted at their ratification conventions that the powers of government be kept separate. They wanted that principle added to the Bill of Rights. After the new government began in 1789, Congress compiled a list of amendments to the Constitution, including this provision: "The powers delegated by this constitution are appropriated to the departments to which they are respectively distributed: so that the legislative department shall never exercise the powers vested in the executive or judicial, nor the executive exercise the powers vested in the legislative or judicial, nor the judicial exercise the powers vested in the legislative or executive departments."[12]

Had this language been adopted, it would not have affected the overlapping of powers already sanctioned by the Constitution. It would not have altered the essential dependence on checks and balances. The separation clause was among 17 amendments sent by the House to the Senate, where it was struck from the list on September 7, 1789. A substitute amendment (to make the three departments "separate and distinct" and to assure that the legislative and executive departments would be restrained from oppression by "feeling and participating the public burthens" through regular elections) failed also. The House and the Senate met in conference to reconcile their two versions. The conferees reduced the list from 17 to 12. Among the deleted amendments was the separation clause.

What would keep the three branches separate and remain faithful to the powers defined in the Constitution? Each branch could be expected to push the limits of their assigned powers and encroach on others. Madison explained in Federalist No. 48 that "a mere demarcation on parchment of the constitutional limits of the several departments is not a sufficient guard against those encroachments which lead to a tyrannical concentration of all the powers of government in the same hands."

Madison held firm to certain constitutional principles. He noted in Federalist No. 49 that "the people are the only legitimate foundation of power." Although he expressed concern about the tendency of republican governments to permit aggrandizement by the legislative department, he did not hesitate in Federalist No. 51 to conclude that in republican government "the legislative authority necessarily predominates." Legislative abuse, he said, would be checked initially to some degree by dividing Congress into two chambers.

As to the future of the republic, Madison left it to the three branches to protect their powers. He advised in Federalist No.

51 that the great safeguard against a gradual concentration of power in a single department "consists in giving those who administer each department the necessary constitutional means and personal motives to resist encroachments of the others. . . . Ambition must be made to counteract ambition. The interest of the man must be connected with the constitutional rights of the place." Over the last 200 years, the presidency and the judiciary have been effective not only in protecting their branches but in extending their powers. Congress was coequal over most of that period, but in the last seven decades it has in large part allowed its powers to decline, partly for refusing to fight off encroachments and in some cases by taking the initiative to surrender power. That pattern will be explored in Chapter 5.

It is tempting to say that if Congress does not protect itself, the fault is its own and it deserves no sympathy or support. The deeper problem is that a decline in the power of Congress is a decline in the power of the people that the legislative branch represents. What is meant by republican government or a "republic"? If you asked that question today you would likely receive puzzled expressions. The framers knew the meaning of a republic and were willing to fight and die for it. A republic is a form of government in which the supreme power rests with the people, exercised through representatives. The value of a republic appears in the Pledge of Allegiance: "I pledge allegiance to the flag of the United States of America and to the Republic for which it stands." The overriding value is not the flag. It is the republic. If the republic disappears, the flag stands for nothing.

Democracy on Trial

The first decade of the new government, beginning in 1789, put democracy and popular control (with a limited franchise) to a severe test. The struggles during this period reaffirm Madison's insight that one should put modest faith in a written constitution. Words can be high sounding and inspiring but meaningless in practice. What matters is the willingness of citizens to defend their rights, often at great cost to themselves. What happens in a democracy when a group uses its power to subjugate others?

Madison anticipated that problem in Federalist No. 10 when he spoke about factions. By that term he meant a number of citizens "united and actuated by some common impulse of passion, or of interest, adverse to the rights of other citizens, or to the permanent and aggregate interests of the community." One remedy would be to destroy the liberty of factions to exist and operate. To Madison, that prescription was "worse than the disease." It would be like abolishing oxygen to eliminate the threat of fires. A republic exists to protect liberty, not to crush it. Nor was there any possibility of controlling factions by giving each citizen the same set of opinions. Beyond its impracticality, it too would destroy liberty and individual choice. In a democracy, citizens naturally had different interests and values.

Madison said that if a faction were less than a majority it could be controlled through the regular political process. Suppose the faction formed a majority? If it existed in a small republic, it could use its political power to suppress the rights and liberties of those in the minority. But Madison looked to a country so large that it would contain hundreds of factions, with one neutralizing the other. Also, the popular passion of a faction would be filtered to some extent through elected representatives and the compromises and accommodations that are part of the political process. The danger of factions could thus be controlled without resorting to punishment, suppression, or expulsion of an unpopular faction. Madison's model worked well in some cases but failed in 1798 when Congress passed the Alien and Sedition Acts, discussed later in this chapter.

In 1792, Congress passed legislation to create a uniform militia drawn from the states. The purpose was to give the country a capacity to suppress insurrections and repel invasions, but lawmakers understood that an abusive militia could also turn itself against the community and threaten individual rights. To guard against ill-use, Congress authorized the president to call up the militia, subject to two checks: the state legislature or the governor had to request assistance, and a Supreme Court justice or district judge had to notify the president.

President George Washington followed those statutory procedures in 1794 when he called up the militia to put down what became known as the Whiskey Rebellion. In 1791, Congress had enacted a federal excise tax on spirits distilled within the United States. Farmers in western Pennsylvania wondered why converting grain into alcohol was taxable and converting grain into flour was not. Federal agents who attempted to collect revenue were tarred and feathered and stripped of horse and money. Opposition to the tax resulted in several deaths, the capture of a federal marshal, and the destruction of property by fire. Justice James Wilson presented to President Washington a certification that state officials were unable to control the rebellion. Washington called up the militias from four states to put down the resisters. Several were tried and convicted.

Washington learned that citizens were holding "certain irregular meetings" to discuss government policies. In Pennsylvania and in other states, citizens formed political clubs and "democratic societies" to meet regularly and debate public issues. Today we would be pleased when citizens take an active interest in government and are willing to attend meetings to express their views. Washington, however, found the meetings offensive and dangerous. He asked: "can any thing be more absurd, more arrogant, or more pernicious to the peace of Society, than for self-created bodies, forming themselves into *permanent* Censors, and under the shade of Night in a concave," especially when they met to criticize statutes that Congress had passed.[13]

In Madison's framework, Washington viewed these self-created societies as "factions" intent on doing harm to the community. Unlike Madison, Washington was not willing to wait for factions to neutralize one another or be curbed by the majority. Washington recognized that all citizens had a constitutional right to petition the government, but he thought that meeting in secret and quite likely without accurate information posed a threat to society. Unless government was willing to intervene and control these meetings, "there is an end of and we may bid adieu to all government in this Country, except Mob and Club Govt. from whence nothing but anarchy and confusion can ensue."[14]

Critics of political clubs saw them as the type of Jacobin societies in Paris that had helped foment the French Revolution. Some members of Washington's cabinet agreed that prompt and decisive action was needed to suppress these organizations. Secretary of State Edmund Randolph advised Washington that he "never did see an opportunity of destroying these self-constituted bodies, until the fruit of their operations was discharged in the insurrection."[15] Now was the time for them to "be crushed."

It was the practice of early presidents to submit an annual message. On November 19, 1794, Washington reviewed the Whiskey Rebellion and the steps he had taken to bring it under control. He singled out for criticism "certain self-created societies" and urged Congress "to turn the machinations of the wicked to the confirming of our constitution: to enable us at all times to root out internal sedition, and put invasion to flight."[16] A very heavy word: *sedition*. For Washington, anyone who attended a meeting and criticized government policy was guilty of sedition, which generally meant open resistance to government authority. A sedition law with criminal penalties appeared four years later.

The Senate quickly praised Washington for his condemnation of self-created societies. In contrast, the House of Representatives spent five full days debating that part of his message. William Smith warned that if the House failed to rush to Washington's defense it "would be an avowed desertion of the Executive."[17] This was an extraordinary argument. If a president made a public statement, each chamber of Congress had a bounden duty to announce its support; otherwise it would be "desertion." The Constitution does not require Congress to walk in lockstep with the president. Each lawmaker is expected to exercise independent thought, as are constituents.

Several members denied they had any obligation to salute whatever a president said. John Nichols asked whether he was expected to "abandon my independence for the sake of the president."[18] If Washington's advisers put him in this dilemma, it was their problem (and Washington's), not Congress's. Josiah Parker of Virginia agreed, pointing out that Washington seemed "misinformed." There was no obligation for a lawmaker "to give up his opinions for the sake of any man." Parker knew of self-created societies in his district and defended them. His constituents "love your Government much, but they love their independence more."[19] Here was a ringing endorsement of government by the people, not government over the people.

William Giles, also of Virginia, wondered what benefit could possibly come from rebuking such abstractions as "self-created societies." What was Washington talking about? People who met in the evening to discuss philosophy, religion, or their stamp collection? What possible constitutional authority did the government have to suppress such meetings? For Giles, Congress had no business trying to restrain or direct public opinion. Citizens had every right to discuss whatever they wanted. If a self-created society violated the law, they could be prosecuted. Otherwise, they were at liberty to function as they liked. Citizens had a right to censure government; government did not have a right to censure citizens.

Madison drove home the same points: "When the people have formed a Constitution, they retain those rights which they have not expressly delegated. It is a question whether what is thus retained can be legislated upon."[20] To Madison, Congress had no authority to legislate on personal opinions or the liberties of speech and press. It was false to say that censure by the government is no punishment: "If it falls on classes of individuals, it will be severe punishment." If Congress were to be faithful to the nature of republican government, "we shall find that the censorial power is in the people over the Government and not in the Government over the people."[21]

After lengthy and thoughtful debate, the House decided against a general attack on self-created societies and limited its remarks to the actions of political clubs in four western counties of Pennsylvania. The House expressed its concern about "misrepresentations" by individuals "or combinations of men" that might have provoked the rebellion and regretted that the public order had "suffered so flagrant a violation." The effort by President Washington to single out political societies for wholesale condemnation and to restrict a citizen's right to express opinions about public policy was soundly rejected.

Individual Conscience

Congressional pushback on Washington's attempt to discredit political clubs depended on lawmakers exercising their independent judgment. Government by the people in these early decades assumed that individuals had the capacity to participate actively and independently in public affairs. Consistent with that philosophy were principles derived from the Enlightenment. A successful government nurtured the liberty of the individual to pursue employment, self-education, and the "pursuit of happiness." The emphasis was on pursuit, not attainment. Individuals needed freedom to develop personal thoughts, beliefs, and talents.

Those principles are captured in an essay that Madison published in *The National Gazette*, March 29, 1792. Entitled "Property," it has nothing to do with modern notions of physical property, including homes, cars, and money. Property in its original meaning derived from the Latin *proprius*: that which is one's own. Madison had talked about this form of property in Federalist No. 10, where he spoke of the "diversity in the faculties of men, from which the rights of property originate." The fundamental value was not physical property but the faculties that individuals use in creating property. For that reason the most important function of government was not to protect property. Rather, the "protection of these faculties is the first object of government."

The 1792 essay explains the personal liberties that individuals need to develop to contribute to the larger community. To Madison, property "embraces every thing to which a man may attach a value and have a right; and *which leaves to every one else the like advantage*."[22] One's conscience existed as a natural right, subject to no restrictions. Madison and Jefferson had helped draft the Virginia Statute for Establishing Religious Freedom. Religion and its free exercise was a fundamental human right over which the state could not intrude: "Our rulers can have authority over such natural rights, only as we have submitted them. The rights of conscience we never submitted, we could not submit."[23]

A century earlier, the Dutch philosopher Spinoza had defended the same values. Individuals had the right to think and reason independently. No man's mind, he wrote, "can possibly lie wholly at the disposition of another, for no one can willingly transfer his natural right of free reason and judgment, or be compelled so to do." Any government that attempted to control minds was, by definition, tyrannical. No government could prescribe what was true or false or what opinions were legitimate or not. "All these questions fall within a man's natural right, which he cannot abdicate even with his own consent."[24]

Those themes emerge clearly in Madison's 1792 essay. A man has a property "in his opinions and the free communication of them." He has a property "in his religious opinions, and in the profession and practice dictated by them." He has a property "in the safety and liberty of his person." He has a property "in the free use of his faculties and free choice of the objects on which to employ them. In a word, as a man is said to have a right to his property, he may be equally said to have a property in his rights."

In a concurrence in 1927, Justice Louis Brandeis restated the basic values that make America special. The framers who won independence from England believed that "the final end of the State was to make men free to develop their faculties; and that in its government the deliberative forces should prevail over the arbitrary."[25] The purpose of government was not to crush independent thought but to encourage it. The framers valued liberty "both as an end and as a means. They believed liberty to be the secret of happiness and courage to be the secret of liberty. They believed that freedom to think as you will and to speak as you think are indispensable to the discovery and spread of political truth; that without free speech and assembly discussion would be futile; that with them, discussion affords ordinarily adequate protection against the dissemination of noxious doctrine; that the greatest menace to freedom is an inert people; that public discussion is a political duty; and that this should be a fundamental principle of the American government."[26]

Sedition and Democracy

Washington's suspicion about "disloyal" members of the political community took root a few years later when President John Adams signed the Alien and Sedition Acts. In 1798, pressures mounted for going to war against France. A similar intolerance of individual opinions and independent thought after the terrorist attacks of September 11, 2001, were present during the Adams administration. On September 20, 2001, President George W. Bush said in a message to Congress: "Every nation, in every region, now has a decision to make: Either you are with us, or you are with the terrorists." In 1798, the nation's leading periodical for the Federalist Party, Philadelphia's *Gazette of the United States*, warned: "He that is not for us, is against us."[27] Those who faced repression in 1798 were the foreign born: "enemy aliens" and "alien friends." Individuals subjected to repression after 9/11 were aliens and "enemy combatants," although there was no effort to punish or prosecute general criticism of the war against terrorism.

In 1798, Congress first passed legislation to extend the waiting period for citizenship from 5 years to 14 years. Part of the motivating force was hostility toward foreigners (even if the lawmakers voting for the legislation were from families born abroad!). Much of the incentive behind this legislation consisted of partisan calculation. The Federalists believed that immigrants were more likely to vote for the Republican-Jeffersonian Party.

After enacting the naturalization bill, Congress passed the Alien Friends Act. It made it lawful for the president to deport any alien "he shall judge dangerous to the peace and safety of the United States." Deportation was also justified if the president had "reasonable grounds" to believe that an alien was involved "in any treasonable or secret machinations" against the federal government. Opponents of the bill objected that existing laws were sufficient to deal with anyone who threatened the government. They objected to vague words like "dangerous" and "machinations." They warned that the bill created a despotic political system, placing all legislative, executive, and judicial powers in a single person: the president. Individuals targeted by this legislation had no right to a public trial to be heard by a jury, confrontation with witnesses, or other procedural safeguards.

A separate statute was aimed at "alien enemies." Whenever there was a declared war between the United States and a foreign nation or any threat of military force by that nation, all noncitizen males 14 years or older were subject to removal from the country. There was no need for evidence about disloyalty or improper conduct. Mere identification with an enemy nation was sufficient. The alien had to appear before a federal court. If the court found "sufficient cause" it would order deportation.

The fourth repressive statute was the Sedition Act. Unlike the two alien bills, penalties for seditious activity applied to both aliens and citizens. Individuals could be fined and imprisoned if they wrote or said anything about Congress or the president deemed to be "false, scandalous and malicious," had the intent to "defame" those political institutions or bring them into "contempt or disrepute," "excite" any hatred against them, or "stir up" sedition or act in combination to oppose or resist federal laws or any presidential act to implement those laws. Any criticism of the government could lead to prosecution. The principle of popular government changed to government threatening the sovereign people. The debate on "self-created societies" in 1794, momentarily turned aside, now took the form of federal law. People were not at liberty to censure government; government was free to censure (and imprison) the people.

The Sedition Act authorized individuals to present as part of their defense "the truth of the matter contained in the publication as a libel." In the end, the government would decide what was true and false. The Adams administration, backed by congressional legislation, began to prosecute and intimidate newspapers that were critical of the Federalist Party and its policies. Because of that policy, many people saw government not as the defender of liberty but its enemy. Moreover, most of the newspapers in the country favored the Federalists, not the Jeffersonians. "Friendly" periodicals got a free pass. Their political opinions of support for the Adams administration were safe and protected.

When Thomas Jefferson was elected president, he used his pardon power to relieve those who had been prosecuted and convicted under the Sedition Act. Years later, Congress passed legislation to appropriate funds to reimburse individuals who had been fined under the statute. A congressional committee denounced the statute as "unconstitutional, null, and void."[28] In *New York Times Co. v. Sullivan* (1964), the Supreme Court acknowledged that the Sedition Act was not struck down by a court of law but by the "court of history." The decisive judgment came not from the judiciary but from a newly elected administration and the general public.

One of the casualties of the war against France in 1798 was John Fries. In order to finance the war, the Federalists enacted a direct tax against homes and improved farmlands. Just as rebels in western Pennsylvania had opposed the excise tax on alcohol, so did Fries and his supporters in eastern Pennsylvania decide they had an obligation and a freedom as citizens to oppose the war tax imposed by the Federalists. Thousands of German American citizens interpreted the tax as a measure designed to drive them into poverty. Believing that resistance to the tax was part of popular sovereignty, they raised "liberty poles" to highlight their opposition. Although John Fries had joined the militia to fight against the Whiskey Rebellion, he now decided to take a stand against his government.

Fries and several hundred supporters marched into Bethlehem, Pennsylvania, to demand the release of men jailed for resisting the tax. They thought the march was consistent with the spirit of the American Revolution and the Constitution, even though they used the threat of force to free the prisoners. To them it was a modest rebellion, at most punishable for inciting a riot or kidnapping federal prisoners. To the Federalists it smacked of sedition and an act of war against the government that satisfied the constitutional language on treason: "Treason against the United States shall consist only in Levying War against them, or in adhering to their Enemies, giving them Aid and Comfort. No Person shall be convicted of Treason unless on the Testimony of two Witnesses to the same overt Act, or in Confession in open Court."

A number of the marchers were found guilty of lesser crimes, fined, and given prison sentences. Fries and two of his colleagues were found guilty of treason ("levying war") and sentenced to be hanged. Gallows were constructed. Shortly before the planned execution President Adams pardoned all three.[29] Enactment of the alien and sedition legislation, the prosecution of Fries and his colleagues, and other national policies helped cripple the Federalist Party. It became identified with elitism and hostility to popular government, public debate, free press, dissent, and civil liberties. After the Jeffersonians won the 1800 elections, the Federalists never again controlled the presidency or Congress. Gradually, the Federalist Party disappeared as a political force.

Free Speech in Wartime

Writing in 1927, Justice Brandeis warned that political order could not be secured "merely through fear of punishment for its infraction; that it is hazardous to discourage thought, hope and imagination; that fear breeds repression; that repression breeds hate; that hate menaces stable government; that the path to safety lies in the opportunity to discuss supposed grievances and proposed remedies."[30] Democracy depended on the power of reason and public discussion. As Brandeis noted, the framers "eschewed silence coerced by law—the argument of force in its worst form."

Yet America has several times passed sedition laws to intimidate and punish citizens who thought in ways the government disliked. It is remarkable in a system of self-government that there should ever be a law of sedition. Citizens go to the polls to elect representatives to protect their rights. At times these representatives have passed laws to imprison individuals who speak or write in a manner objectionable to the government. Criticism of government, no matter how informed and responsible, is equated with "disloyalty." Understandably, attempts to overthrow government must be met by force. No such threat comes from those who simply criticize government. The threat comes in trying to repress them.

Under royal government, citizens had no right to say the king was wrong or utter any misgivings, no matter how mildly or cautiously expressed. Similarly, a sedition statute makes it a crime to find fault with the president, Congress, or the Supreme Court. Under either system, the individual is subordinate to those who exercise power. Patriots often say: "my country, right or wrong." During congressional debate in 1872, Senator Carl Schurz presented a more thoughtful and independent position: "My country, right or wrong; if right, to be kept right; and if wrong, to be set right."[31]

At hearings in 1987, Senator George Mitchell reflected on his service as a federal judge. He asked immigrants, about to take their oath to become U.S. citizens, why they came to America. Those who fled from totalitarian or repressive systems said, "We came here because here in America you can criticize the government without looking over your shoulder." They valued the individual freedom to disagree with public authorities. Mitchell emphasized that disagreement with government "was not evidence of lack of patriotism."[32] More recently, when critics of the Iraq War were attacked as unpatriotic in 2005, Senator Chuck Hagel advised: "[t]o question your government is not unpatriotic—to *not* question your government is unpatriotic."[33]

As with the Quasi-War against France in 1798, sedition laws generally appear when the nation faces an outside enemy or the government decides that prosecuting "seditionists" will yield partisan benefits. During the War of 1812, Jeffersonians did not enact a federal sedition law but nevertheless were willing to prosecute newspapers owned by Federalists. Jeffersonians relied not on a sedition statute but on the law of "seditious libel" borrowed from British law. This period is described in greater detail in Chapter 3.

In 1917, after the United States had entered into World War I, several states passed sedition legislation. One individual was prosecuted and convicted under a Minnesota law for remarking in public: "We were stampeded into this war by newspaper rot to pull England's chestnuts out of the fire."[34] Congress used the Montana sedition act as a model. With only the change of three words it became the federal sedition statute of 1918. It covered anyone who "shall willfully utter, print, write, or publish any disloyal, profane, scurrilous, or abusive language" about the form of the U.S. government, the U.S. Constitution, military or naval forces, the U.S. flag, or the uniform of the army or the navy, or use any language intended to bring the U.S. government, the Constitution, or U.S. armed forces "into contempt, scorn, contumely, or disrepute." The penalties: a fine of $10,000 and 20 years in prison, or both. How could prosecutors and judges possibly understand and apply such words as "scurrilous"? In the 1940 Smith Act, Congress adopted legislation to punish seditious utterances. The statute did not use the word *sedition*, but the government nonetheless proceeded to hold sedition trials.[35]

Should free speech be permitted in time of war? May citizens in a republic express their views? During World War I, justices of the Supreme Court reasoned that whatever rights of free speech and free press exist during peacetime, those freedoms are properly circumscribed when the country is at war. In a major case in 1919, Justice Oliver Wendell Holmes offered a famous analogy: "The most stringent protection of free speech would not protect a man in falsely shouting fire in a theater and causing a panic."[36] At issue in this case was the conviction of opponents of the war who mailed printed circulars intended to obstruct the recruitment of U.S. soldiers. What does shouting fire in a crowded theater have to do with circulating a leaflet that expresses an *opinion*? Citizens in a democratic country should be at liberty to express their views about the nation's commitment to war. They pay for it and provide the soldiers.

In the June 1919 issue of *Harvard Law Review*, Professor Zechariah Chafee Jr. rejected the theory that individual rights to speak and write about government policies are restricted in time of war. Under his analysis, the First Amendment applies in time of peace and war. Citizens are entitled to engage in broad debate about national policies. Chafee defended two interests: the right of an individual to express opinions and the need of society to hear and consider criticism. Raising objections is not seditious; it is a citizen's duty. Chafee noted that the framers who drafted the Bill of Rights, including the First Amendment, had just been through a war. It was especially in time of military emergencies that citizens need to speak out freely, because it is during such periods that government can inflict the greatest damage on constitutional rights. War brings burdens and sacrifices, including financial costs, military service, combat deaths, and casualties. The rights of speech and press during that period should be unimpaired.

To defend the American value of popular sovereignty and the system of checks and balances, Congress needs to assert its ample powers. Our liberties depend on independent lawmakers able and willing to correct presidential and judicial mistakes. The next two chapters examine the record of Congress in pushing back against the other branches and protecting the rights of citizens.

CHAPTER TWO
FACING EXECUTIVE POWER

The framers looked to Congress as the first branch of government. Its powers appear in Article I of the Constitution. By contrast, reading the debates at the Philadelphia Convention provides little insight into what the delegates expected of presidential power. Beyond the executive powers listed in Article II, there is barely a glimpse of how the office of the president might evolve. The only express presidential power associated with the British king is the power to pardon, an act of grace and mercy that emerged centuries ago. Other presidential duties have British precedents: receiving ambassadors and serving as commander in chief.

Presidents have over the years claimed "emergency" and "inherent" powers that seem close cousin to monarchical powers. Unfortunately, some scholars have encouraged this trend, even if they later expressed regret for giving encouragement to illegal and abusive executive actions. For its part, Congress has failed to consistently check presidential excesses that threaten constitutional government and the rights and liberties of individuals. What are the legitimate sources of presidential power? Where does danger lie?

Enumerated Powers Only?

On several occasions the Supreme Court has announced that the authority of the national government is defined by enumerated powers. Consider the Court's claim in 1995: "We start with first principles. The Constitution creates a Federal Government of enumerated powers." Two years later the Court stated: "Under our Constitution, the Federal Government is one of enumerated powers."[1] It is doubtful that a single framer had that understanding of the Constitution. If each branch possessed only powers specifically enumerated, the Court would have no power of judicial review, a power that is not expressly stated in the Constitution. Many other federal powers routinely exercised today (and even from the start) are not expressly stated in that document.

The Articles of Confederation attempted to confine government to enumerated powers. The states retained all powers except those "expressly delegated" to the national government. In 1791, during debate on the Tenth Amendment, it was proposed that the same language be used to limit the national government. Powers not "expressly delegated" to the national government would be reserved to the states or to the people. Madison strongly objected to limiting the federal government to express powers. He said the functions and responsibilities of government could not be delineated with such precision. It was impossible to confine a government to the exercise of express powers, for there "must necessarily be admitted powers by implication, unless the Constitution descended to recount every minutia."[2] Congress deleted "expressly" from the Tenth Amendment.

It is often claimed that Congress is restricted to enumerated powers but the president is not. Here is the argument. Article I of the Constitution begins: "All legislative Powers herein granted shall be vested in a Congress of the United States, which shall consist of a Senate and House of Representatives." The words "herein granted" do not appear in Article II: "The executive Power shall be vested in a President." From that language it is reasoned that Congress possesses only those powers specifically granted, whereas the president has the whole of the "executive Power" (powers specifically stated plus unnamed powers customarily associated with the executive).

As explained in one study, the president's powers "go beyond those specifically enumerated in Article II, Sections 2 and 3, and include at least some implied, residual executive powers, like the removal power, as well."[3] It is quite true that presidents have implied powers that can be reasonably drawn from express powers. Presidents have the express duty under the Constitution to see that the laws are faithfully executed and may therefore remove an executive official (including a department head) who interferes with the execution of a law. But implied powers are not unique to the president. They are available to the other branches. Congress has the express power to legislate. To legislate in an informed manner, it has the implied power to investigate, issue subpoenas, and hold executive officials and private citizens in contempt. To assure that statutes are being properly implemented, Congress has the implied power to conduct oversight of executive agencies and seek agency documents and testimony.

There is a second reason why congressional powers are not confined to powers expressly stated in Article I. It is what is called the Necessary and Proper Clause. Consider the breadth of this constitutional grant of power to Congress: "To make all Laws which shall be necessary and proper for carrying into Execution the foregoing [express] Powers, and all other Powers vested by this Constitution in the Government of the United States, or in any Department or Officer thereof." This provision has been interpreted over the years to grant Congress broad authority, not only over its own powers but extending to powers vested in "any Department or Officer thereof." In the celebrated case of *McCulloch v. Maryland* (1819), Chief Justice John Marshall offered a generous interpretation of congressional power under the clause: "Let the end be legitimate, let it be within the scope of the constitution, and all means which are appropriate, which are plainly adapted to that end, which are not prohibited, but consist with the letter and spirit of the constitution, are constitutional."[4]

Operating Under the Prerogative

Beyond express and implied powers, presidents have exercised what has been called the "prerogative." In his *Second Treatise on Government* (1690), the British philosopher John Locke anticipated situations in which an executive must be at liberty to protect the community, with or without law. The power to act "according to discretion for the public good, without the prescription of the law and sometimes against it, is that which is called prerogative." The only limit placed by Locke on executive discretion was to act for the good of the people and not against it. In cases where the legislature or the people questioned the necessity or propriety of executive action, "there can be no judge on earth." The sole remedy: an "appeal to Heaven."

The American framers did not look to the skies to control executive abuse. If presidents decided to act in the absence of law or against it, they had to come to Congress and seek legislative authority, even if applied retroactively. After Congress had recessed in 1807, a British vessel fired on the American ship Chesapeake. Jefferson responded by ordering military purchases and reported his actions to Congress. He reasoned: "To have awaited a previous and special sanction by law would have lost occasions which might not be retrieved."[5] Congressional adjournments at that time were for much longer periods than today, especially in the second session. If Congress decided that Jefferson's initiative violated law or was abusive, it could act against him by withholding funds or setting in motion an impeachment trial. The president acts outside the law at risk. In Jefferson's case (and others), the remedy is secular, not celestial.

In his years of retirement, Jefferson remarked that observance of the written law is a high duty of a public official but not the highest. A higher priority is the law of self-preservation: "To lose our country by a scrupulous adherence to written law, would be to lose the law itself, with life, liberty, property and all those who are enjoying them with us; thus absurdly sacrificing the end to the means."[6] This version of the prerogative aims at national survival. Under this interpretation, the president's express power to see that the laws are faithfully executed might be waived in an emergency.

That precise condition faced President Abraham Lincoln in April 1861, when Congress was out of session. Responding to confederate attacks on Ft. Sumter in South Carolina, he issued proclamations calling forth the militia, withdrawing funds from the treasury without an appropriation, placing a blockade on the rebellious states, and suspending the writ of habeas corpus. In taking those emergency actions, he never claimed to possess authority to do what he did. He explained to Congress when it returned that his actions "whether strictly legal or not" were undertaken as a public necessity, "trusting then, as now, that Congress would readily ratify them."[7]

In other public messages Lincoln said he exercised the "war power," by which he meant whatever he had under Article II plus whatever legislative powers Congress had under Article I. As noted in his message, he believed his actions were not "beyond the constitutional competency of Congress." He therefore admitted to using congressional powers and understood he had to come to Congress, present his case, and ask for a statute to approve and legalize his actions, as though they had been done under the express authority and direction of Congress. In debating his request, lawmakers voted with the understanding that Lincoln exceeded his constitutional authority. Congress passed the bill and presented it to Lincoln for his signature. Through this conduct Lincoln preserved both the Union and the Constitution.

Those who believe the president may go to war without seeking authority from Congress frequently cite the Supreme Court's decision in *The Prize Cases* (1863), which upheld Lincoln's blockade in the South. However, Lincoln and his advisers never argued that he could take unilateral military actions against other nations without first coming to Congress for approval. In the 1863 case, Justice Robert Grier specifically denied that the president as commander in chief had any authority to initiate war against another country. What was at stake in the case was a domestic matter: civil war. It was internal, not external. Lincoln acted defensively, not offensively. Grier plainly stated that the president "has no power to initiate or declare a war either against a foreign nation or a domestic State." The executive branch agreed. During oral argument, the attorney representing the president acknowledged that Lincoln's actions had nothing to do with "the right *to initiate a war, as a voluntary act of sovereignty*. That is vested only in Congress."[8]

Upping the Ante: Inherent Powers

Beyond implied powers and the prerogative (yet often confused with each) is the claim that the president possesses certain "inherent powers." Here one needs to repair to the dictionary to understand terms. The fifth edition of *Black's Law Dictionary* gives this account of *inherent*: "An authority possessed without its being derived from another. . . . Powers over and beyond those explicitly granted in the Constitution or reasonably to be implied from express powers." Inherent is clearly set apart from express and implied powers. That definition remained in the sixth edition. The eighth edition, published in 2004, contains different language: "A power that necessarily derives from an office, position, or status." Again, the authority is not express or implied. It exists somewhere in the nature of the office or person.

The purpose of a constitution is to limit government to preserve a realm of individual freedom. Express and implied powers serve that objective. Inherent powers do not. They are too open-ended. What "inheres" in the president? The standard collegiate dictionary explains that *inherent* covers the "essential character of something: belonging by nature or habit." That is much too vague and uncertain for a constitutional system. Who knows what is essential or belongs to nature? Dictionaries cross-reference *inherent* to *intrinsic*, which means something within a body (as distinct from extrinsic). It belongs "to the essential nature or constitution of a thing." Such words as *inherent*, *essential*, *nature*, and *intrinsic* open the door to broad executive powers that are destructive of a constitutional order and threaten individual liberties.

Also falling within the category of inherent power is the claim that the president functions as "sole organ" in foreign affairs. In *United States v. Curtiss-Wright* (1936),[9] the Supreme Court upheld a congressional grant of power to the president in international relations. The power delegated was exclusively legislative, not executive, yet Justice George Sutherland devoted pages of dicta (extraneous matter) to claim that the president possesses plenary and unchecked powers in foreign affairs. He cited this statement by John Marshall when he served as a member of the House of Representatives in 1800: "The President is the sole organ of the nation in its external relations, and its sole representative with foreign nations."[10]

The "sole organ" doctrine has been cited ever since to justify presidential actions even when they violate statutes and treaties. A recent example of invoking that doctrine is the defense of secret surveillance by the National Security Agency (NSA) after 9/11, despite enactment of the Foreign Intelligence Surveillance Act (FISA) that requires warrants from a court. The Justice Department concluded that the NSA program was constitutional because the president may exercise "well-recognized inherent constitutional authority as Commander in Chief and sole organ for the Nation in foreign affairs to conduct warrantless surveillance of enemy forces for intelligence purposes to detect and disrupt armed attacks on the United States."[11] Some case law can be read to support presidential action outside of FISA, but the argument is strained and unpersuasive.[12]

When one reads the congressional debate in 1800 it is obvious that Marshall never claimed for the president any authority to act outside the law. At no time in his lengthy public service as secretary of state, member of Congress, or chief justice of the United States, did he ever come close to supporting such a doctrine. What was debated in 1800 was whether Congress should censure or impeach President John Adams for handing over to England a person charged with murder. Some lawmakers condemned Adams for invading the powers of the judiciary.

It was at that point that Marshall took the floor to argue that there were no grounds for taking any punitive action against the president. What Adams had done was to fulfill his constitutional duty to see that the laws be faithfully executed. The law was the Jay Treaty. Article 27 provided that the United States and Great Britain would deliver up to each other "all persons" charged with murder or forgery. Marshall was not arguing for any kind of inherent or exclusive executive power, much less a power that found its existence outside the Constitution. Adams was simply carrying out a treaty. He was not the sole organ in formulating the treaty. He was the sole organ in *implementing* it. Article II states that it is the president's duty to "take Care that the Laws be faithfully executed." Article VI provides that all treaties "shall be the supreme Law of the Land." Only after government policy had been established through the collective action of the executive and legislative branches, either by treaty or statute, did the president emerge as the sole organ in implementing national policy.

Later, as chief justice of the Supreme Court, Marshall held firm to his position that the making of foreign policy is a joint exercise by the executive and legislative branches. Unlike England and the British royal prerogative, as set forth by William Blackstone in his *Commentaries*, the U.S. president did not enjoy plenary and exclusive power over foreign affairs and the war power. With the war power, Marshall looked solely to Congress—not the president—for authority to take the country to war: "The whole powers of war being, by the constitution of the United States, vested in congress, the acts of that body can alone be resorted to as our guides in this enquiry."[13]

An 1804 opinion by Marshall underscores the degree to which the United States had broken free of royal authority over foreign affairs and war. At the start of the Quasi-War against France, Congress passed legislation to authorize the president to seize vessels sailing *to* French ports. President Adams exceeded the statute by ordering American ships to capture vessels sailing *to or from* French ports. A U.S. naval captain was sued for violating the statute. Initially, Marshall thought that the captain's action was appropriate because he had followed the instructions of his superior, the president. Marshall, however, concluded that the president "cannot change the nature of the transaction, or legalize an act which, without those instructions, would have been a plain trespass."[14] Even when a president issues an order as commander in chief in time of war, an action contrary to statutory policy is invalid under the Constitution.

Exercising Inherent Powers

Anyone who studies the use of inherent presidential power will find that these claims of plenary and exclusive authority are regularly met and defeated by congressional and judicial action. One example is the decision by President Harry Truman to seize steel mills in 1952 to prosecute the war in Korea. By that time the war was extremely unpopular in the United States because of lives lost, fortunes spent, and little hope of military victory. Americans did not "rally round the president." Instead of exercising existing statutory authority to place an 80-day cooling-off period on the pending strike by labor unions, Truman chose to act independently by invoking broad emergency authority.

The Justice Department made things worse in court by defending his action solely on the basis of inherent executive power. The attorney handling the case for the administration told the trial judge that courts were powerless to control this exercise of presidential power. To the attorney, only two limits on presidential power existed: the ballot box and impeachment.

The trial judge inquired whether when the sovereign people ratified the Constitution "it limited Congress, it limited the judiciary, but did not limit the executive." Unfazed, the attorney responded: "That's our conception, Your Honor." The judge probed further, asking whether once the president determines that an emergency exists, "the courts cannot even review whether it is an emergency." Back came the confident reply: "That is correct."[15]

This theory of presidential power backfired. Reporters asked Truman, if he could seize steel mills, could he also seize newspapers and radio stations? He said that under the Constitution the president could do whatever he thought best for the country. Editorials around the country condemned him for acting unconstitutionally and for trying to wield dictatorial powers. The trial judge issued an injunction to stop the steel seizure, releasing a blistering opinion that shredded the administration's claim of inherent and emergency powers for the president. The administration had proposed a form of government "alien to our Constitutional government of limited powers."[16] The judge acknowledged that a nationwide strike could do extensive damage to the country, but concluded that a strike "would be less injurious to the public than the injury which would flow from a timorous judicial recognition that there is some basis for this claim to unlimited and unrestrained Executive power, which would be implicit in a failure to grant the injunction."[17] The Supreme Court, divided six to three, upheld the trial court.[18]

The Nixon administration argued that the president had inherent authority not to spend appropriated funds. In what became known as the impoundment dispute, President Nixon proceeded to cut programs in half and even eliminate them. Congress held hearings to explore the legal basis for this theory. Litigation led to about 80 cases, with the administration losing all but 2 or 3 and losing the 1 case that reached the Supreme Court. After several years of confrontation, Nixon agreed to sign the Impoundment Control Act of 1974, establishing restrictions on efforts to temporarily slow down a program or terminate funding entirely. What began as a claim of unlimited presidential power ended with the acceptance of statutory restraints.

I was fortunate to have a front-row seat to this battle. Because of two articles I had published on the impoundment issue, Senator Sam J. Ervin Jr. invited me to work with his Subcommittee on Separation of Powers. I sat behind him at hearings to provide professional counsel, sat next to him at committee markup to offer views on amendments submitted to the draft bill, wrote the conference report, and prepared a "dialogue" between Senator Ervin and Senator Hubert Humphrey that went into the *Congressional Record* to explain the intent of the bill. I received a letter from President Nixon, dated July 22, 1974, because of my "special interest in this legislation." The package included a ceremonial signing pen.[19]

Nixon also claimed inherent authority to conduct warrantless domestic surveillance. He lost in court at every level: federal district court, the Court of Appeals for the Sixth Circuit, and the Supreme Court. The Sixth Circuit, in *United States v. United States District Court* (1971), remarked: "It is strange, indeed, that in this case the traditional power of sovereigns like King George III should be invoked on behalf of an American President to defeat one of the fundamental freedoms for which the founders of this country overthrew King George's reign."[20] Unanimously, the Supreme Court affirmed the Sixth Circuit. This litigation focused on domestic surveillance. Congress later passed legislation to limit presidential authority in the field of national security surveillance (the Foreign Intelligence Surveillance Act of 1978).

Following the terrorist attacks of 9/11, President George W. Bush invoked inherent powers in several areas. He issued a military order on November 13, 2001, to authorize military tribunals for noncitizens who belonged to al Qaeda, engaged in international terrorism, or harbored such individuals. The Justice Department pointed to statutory authority to justify his action but also insisted that the president had inherent authority to convene the tribunals, even in the absence of specific congressional authority. Bush's initiative represented a "core exercise of the president's commander-in-chief and foreign affairs powers during wartime and is entitled to be given effect by the courts."[21] In 2006, the Supreme Court in *Hamdan v. Rumsfeld* found that argument without merit. No such inherent, Article II authority existed. It was necessary for President Bush to seek legislation, which passed in the form of the Military Commissions Act.[22]

Similarly, the administration argued that President Bush possessed constitutional authority to designate U.S. citizens (Yaser Esam Hamdi and Jose Padilla) as "enemy combatants" and hold them incommunicado year after year without access to an attorney or trial. The Justice Department advised courts not to interfere with presidential decisions in this area, insisting that the Constitution vests the president "with exclusive authority to act as commander in chief and as the nation's sole organ in foreign affairs."[23] Courts should not try to "second-guess" presidential judgments and intrude upon "the constitutional prerogative of the commander in chief." In 2004, eight justices of the Supreme Court rejected the administration's central argument that the detention of a U.S. citizen was quintessentially a presidential decision. Justice O'Connor announced in *Hamdi v. Rumsfeld*: "We necessarily reject the Government's assertion that separation of powers principles mandate a heavily circumscribed role for the courts in such circumstances. . . . Whatever power the United States Constitution envisions for the Executive in its exchanges with other nations or with enemy organizations in times of conflict, it most assuredly envisions a role for all three branches when individual liberties are at stake."[24]

Legal memos produced in the Bush administration concluded that terrorist suspects picked up in Afghanistan, Pakistan, and other countries could be held indefinitely at the U.S. naval base at Guantánamo Bay, Cuba, without interference by the judiciary. The naval base, according to the administration, was outside the United States and therefore beyond the jurisdiction of federal judges. The United States occupies the base under a lease entered into with the Cuban government in 1903 and exercises complete jurisdiction and control over the property. In court, the administration argued that the base was nonetheless beyond the jurisdiction of courts because the United States did not possess "sovereignty" over the area. Cuba did. That defense of presidential discretion was rejected by the Supreme Court in *Rasul v. Bush* (2004).[25] Four years later, in *Boumediene v. Bush*,[26] the Court again insisted that federal courts had a role to play in resolving the issues of detainees held at the naval base.

Finally, the Bush administration decided to violate FISA and secretly conduct warrantless surveillance. A primary part of the FISA statute is the requirement that executive officials must first obtain a warrant from a specially created court. When the project was revealed by the *New York Times* in December 2005, the administration relied in part on inherent presidential powers in its defense. Private parties filed many court cases to challenge NSA surveillance. After much activity by all three branches, the administration came to Congress and obtained statutory authority.[27]

Championing the Imperial Presidency

The framers understood that all three branches would attempt to expand their powers. Checks and balances were available to fight off encroachments. It is unlikely that any framer could have anticipated that scholars would later throw their weight wholly behind presidential power and dismiss legislative and judicial constraints. Especially after World War II, historians, political scientists, and law professors placed the president on a pedestal and attributed to that office a host of wondrous qualities. Scholars expected occupants of the Oval Office to act invariably for the "national interest" on the basis of unrivaled expertise and benevolent intentions. Political idolatry of any stripe, including the divine right of kings or waiting for a Great Man, found no support among the framers. They did not put their faith in a single person. Fearing concentrated power, they believed in process and structural checks.

The framers were well aware that British precedents assigned all of external affairs, including the war power, to the king. William Blackstone in his *Commentaries* treated all of foreign affairs and the war power as monarchical: the power to declare war, make treaties, appoint ambassadors, order reprisals (small wars), and issue letters of marque (authorizing private citizens to contribute ships and other property for military operations). Under the U.S. Constitution, those powers were either given expressly to Congress in Article I or shared between the president and the Senate (treaties and appointments). Not one of those powers was vested exclusively with the president. The framers broke decisively with the English and Blackstone model.

In June 1950, President Truman went to war against North Korea without ever coming to Congress for authority. It was the first time that a president had ever unilaterally committed the nation to a major war without first seeking legislative authority. For 160 years presidents regularly came to Congress to request either a declaration or authorization for significant military commitments. The academic community in 1950 had an opportunity to challenge Truman's actions and remind him and the public of fundamental constitutional values. Instead, prominent scholars and professors rushed to his defense and concocted feeble arguments they would later regret and retract.

The historian Henry Steele Commager rebuked the critics of Truman's intervention in Korea, briskly stating that their objections "have no support in law or in history." Supremely confident of his understanding, the matter seemed "so hackneyed a theme that even politicians might reasonably be expected to be familiar with it."[28] Commager cited precedents from a number of presidents but not a single one came close to justifying Truman's action. Commager believed that strong presidents may act boldly without any threat to democracy or the constitutional system. There were no grounds, he advised, for distrusting executive authority. What had happened to scholarly appreciation for separation of powers, checks and balances, and concerns about political mistakes and abuse?

Less than two decades later, with the country mired in a bitter war in Southeast Asia, Commager publicly apologized for his earlier unrestrained enthusiasm for presidential power. In testimony before the Senate Foreign Relations Committee in 1967 he urged a reconsideration of executive-legislative relations in the field of foreign affairs and the war power. Four years later he told the committee that "it is very dangerous to allow the president to, in effect, commit us to a war from which we cannot withdraw, because the war-making power is lodged and was intended to be lodged in the Congress." Had he just learned that? Probably not. More likely he decided in 1950 to remove his academic hat and don a partisan one.

Another major supporter of Truman's military action in Korea was the historian Arthur M. Schlesinger Jr. In the past he had written a number of books extolling the virtues and strengths of such presidents as Andrew Jackson and Franklin D. Roosevelt. He wrote another glowing tribute to John F. Kennedy. He remained a presidency man with little regard for or understanding of constitutional limits and checks. The more power concentrated in the president, the better. Ironically, after this pattern of hagiographic studies about executive power he would publish a critique in 1973 called *The Imperial Presidency*. He had done much to defend imperial pretensions.

In 1950, at the start of the Korean War, Schlesinger issued a public attack on Senator Robert Taft for saying that Truman "had no authority whatever to commit American troops to Korea without consulting Congress and without congressional approval."[29] Taft charged that Truman had usurped authority and violated statutes and the Constitution. Schlesinger dismissed Taft's analysis as "demonstrably irresponsible." He issued a stern rebuke: "Until Senator Taft and his friends succeed in rewriting American history according to their own specifications these facts must stand as obstacles to their efforts to foist off their current political prejudices as eternal American verities."[30]

There were indeed demonstrably irresponsible statements and foisting off of political prejudices, but they were by Schlesinger—not Taft. The historical examples Schlesinger identified had zero bearing on Truman's claim that he could go to war against another country without first coming to Congress for authority. Presidential scholar Edward S. Corwin reacted to Commager and Schlesinger by criticizing the "course of constitutional development, practical and polemical, which ascribes to the President a truly royal prerogative in the field of foreign relations, and does so without indicating any correlative legal or constitutional control to which he is answerable." Corwin warned: "Our high-flying prerogative men appear to resent the very idea that the only possible source of such control, Congress to wit, has any effective power in the premises at all."[31]

After witnessing the abuse of presidential power in the Vietnam War and the Watergate scandal, Schlesinger publicly apologized in his book, *The Imperial Presidency*, for calling Taft's statement "demonstrably irresponsible." He said that he had responded with "a flourish of historical documentation and, also, hyperbole." His errors went beyond flourishes and hyperbole. The historical documentation he offered had nothing to do with Truman's war in Korea. Unlike Taft, Schlesinger had no constitutional model other than a slavish devotion to presidential power, in this case a convenient one. Truman was a Democrat and Schlesinger remained a party loyalist.

In a book he coauthored with Alfred de Grazia, *Congress and the Presidency* (1967), Schlesinger counseled that "something must be done to assure the Congress a more authoritative and continuing voice in fundamental decisions in foreign policy." In *The Imperial Presidency*, Schlesinger analyzed the domestic and international pressures that helped push power to the presidency: "It must be said that historians and political scientists, this writer among them, contributed to the presidential mystique."[32] Why would a scholar, devoted to his craft, engage in mystery-making? Corwin and other scholars chose not to. It is important for every individual, including famous scholars, to reevaluate and rethink what they have said and written. But independent scholarly analysis is needed at the time of constitutional violations, not two decades later.

Probably no presidential study has been as influential as Richard Neustadt's *Presidential Power* (1960). The book was popular with professors and students because it offered lively case studies and put an emphasis on practical politics. However, entirely missing from the book was anything to do with institutional, legal, or constitutional values. Although the book is often remembered for defining presidential power as "the power to persuade," Neustadt clearly urged presidents to take power, not share it. Political power was something to be acquired and concentrated in the presidency. The power was to be used for *personal* use, not for something more general. He urged presidents to practice the "politics of self-aggrandizement." Because President Dwight D. Eisenhower appeared to care more about national unity than personal power, Neustadt dismissed him as an "amateur."

Among the case studies in the book is the Korean War, including Truman's dismissal of General Douglas MacArthur and the Supreme Court's action in striking down the steel seizure. Not one word was devoted to analyzing Truman's legal and constitutional authority to initiate the war without congressional approval. No attention was given to Truman's inflated definition of emergency power. Certainly he did not practice the politics of "persuasion" to convince Congress and the people about the war. To Neustadt, those issues did not matter. What counted was Truman's intention to make decisions, take initiatives, and be the "man-in-charge." Neustadt's advice: "The more determinedly a President seeks power, the more he will be likely to bring vigor to his clerkship. As he does so he contributes to the energy of government."[33]

Alexander Hamilton and other framers saw the need for "energy" in the executive, but it was energy within the law, not outside it. Otherwise, why would the Constitution direct the president to take care that the laws be faithfully executed? Executive power under the Constitution is more than making decisions, taking initiatives, and bringing vigor and energy to the office. Neustadt provided advice for "a man who seeks to maximize his power." Such a framework describes the administrations of Franklin Roosevelt and Winston Churchill but fits equally well the careers of Adolf Hitler, Benito Mussolini, and Joseph Stalin. One system is constitutional, limited by checks and balances; the other is dictatorial. By wholly ignoring law and the Constitution, Neustadt never distinguished between these competing models of government.[34]

Defenders of Congress

Commager, Schlesinger, and Neustadt wrote and spoke as academic liberals, putting their weight fully behind presidential power. Conservatives in early periods of American history had also supported central power, especially in the executive, to guard against possible dangers and risks from what they feared would be mob democracy. But later they were more likely to endorse an independent Congress and the system of checks and balances, finding safety and protection in decentralized government and the deliberative process. Placing trust in a single official to guide the country did violence to their principles.

Over the past seven decades, critiques of presidential power came typically from scholars who touted conservative or Whiggish views (supportive of legislative power). They were the ones who kept alive the values of republican government. In his classic *The Road to Serfdom* (1944), Friedrich A. Hayek warned about the transfer of legislative power to "experts" in the executive branch. He said the shift posed a threat to democracy and would produce arbitrary power and dictatorship. Conservatives counted Hayek among their ranks, but in a thoughtful article he declined full membership, preferring to classify himself as "an unrepentant Old Whig—with the stress on the 'old.'"[35]

Another conservative, James Burnham, published a full-fledged defense of congressional prerogatives in *Congress and the American Tradition* (1959). He said the framers believed that "in a republican and representative governmental system the preponderating share of power was held and exercised by the legislature."[36] He explained that conservatives favored the relative power of Congress "within the diffused power equilibrium." Liberals tended to distrust Congress and prefer executive power. As to the war power, Burnham concluded that by "the intent of the Founding Fathers and the letter and tradition of the Constitution, the bulk of the sovereign war power was assigned to Congress."[37] Preserving liberty and strengthening a strong legislature were closely linked: "If Congress ceases to be an actively functioning political institution, then political liberty in the United States will soon come to an end."[38]

In 1960, an article by Willmoore Kendall placed a conservative imprimatur on the role of Congress in safeguarding republican government and individual liberties. He listed some conventional generalizations about the virtues of the president and Congress, with the president representing "high principle" and Congress associated with low principle, no principle at all, reaction, and unintelligence. Kendall found those stereotypes not only trite and inaccurate but destructive of the system of checks and balances and constitutional principles.[39]

The conservative American Enterprise Institute sponsored a series of studies edited by Alfred de Grazia and published in 1967. The title left no doubt about the commitment to republican government: *Congress: The First Branch of Government*. De Grazia described Congress as "the central institution of the American democratic republic. Unless it functions well and powerfully, much more so than it has in the past, the road to a bureaucratic state and kind of monarchic government will be opened up."[40] To those who rhapsodized about the coherence, unity, harmony, and rationality of the president, de Grazia reminded them that the president is "a Congress with a skin thrown over him."[41] If you look carefully within the executive branch you will see fragmentation, divisions, compromise, and various interests fighting for control. The difference is that the legislative process is largely visible; the executive process is not.

Ronald Moe published a book of readings in 1971 called *Congress and the President: Allies and Adversaries*. His selections underscored the vital importance of Congress in a constitutional order. He described what seemed to him as the liberals' attraction to the presidency: "Historically, there has been a tendency for intellectuals to be wary of democratic legislatures, and hesitant about the ability of people to completely run their affairs, especially the affairs of state."[42] He noted that liberals concluded that their influence within the executive branch would be greater than in Congress.

Switching Sides

In recent decades, political scientists, historians, and law professors have begun to rethink the scholarly fascination with the presidency. In a paper delivered at the 1970 American Political Science Association annual meeting, Thomas Cronin criticized existing textbooks for promoting "inflated and unrealistic interpretations of presidential competence and beneficence." Scholarly works inclined toward "exaggerations about past and future presidential performance." Infatuation with the presidency necessarily diminishes the importance of Congress, the judiciary, the Constitution, the rule of law, and the democratic process.

Having nourished the "textbook presidency," liberals turned against it for a time because of the Vietnam War and Watergate. Yet some scholars see those periods as mere aberrations, attributable to poor misjudgments by a few occupants of the White House. Taking Vietnam and Watergate as the exception, not the rule, they continued to endorse and teach Neustadt's model of presidential power. Students were taught that American foreign policy and military commitments are dominated by presidents and their advisors, giving little attention to constitutional principles.[43] Admissions of error by Commager and Schlesinger appeared to be mere mid-course corrections of no lasting value.

With liberals reconsidering their views, some conservatives switched course and defended a strong presidency. An article in the *Wall Street Journal* on September 20, 1974, by Irving Kristol was called "The Inexorable Rise of the Executive." Especially in the area of foreign affairs he wanted a strong president. The "imperial presidency," in one form or another, was "here to stay." Conservatives like Kristol looked to threats from the Soviet Union and placed their bets with presidential power. Constitutional values did not matter. To Norman Podhoretz, editor of the conservative magazine *Commentary*, the attacks on the presidency after Vietnam and Watergate damaged "the main institutional capability the United States possesses for conducting an overt fight against the spread of Communist power in the world."[44] For Podhoretz and others, the outside threat of communism justified the abandonment or diminishment of constitutional checks.

Essentially, Kristol, Podhoretz, and other conservatives (later called "neoconservatives") adopted the same position as the liberal trio of Commager, Schlesinger, and Neustadt. Each side calculated which branch would better serve its political agenda or national needs. Neither side paid attention to the Constitution, separation of powers, checks and balances, or the structural principles that provide fundamental safeguards for protecting individual rights. These liberals and conservatives were willing to move the United States toward a centralized political system to counter the power of the Soviet Union.

Conservative scholars in recent decades gave little attention to Congress, other than to write derogatory studies. One example is a book edited by Gordon S. Jones and John A. Marini entitled *The Imperial Congress* (1988). Fortunately, there were exceptions to this pattern, including the works of Joseph Bessette and a volume he edited with Jeffrey Tulis.[45] It was their purpose to assure that the president operates within the constraints of public law, and to that extent they broke decisively with Neustadt, David Barber, and other presidential scholars. Mickey Edwards, former Republican member of the House of Representatives from Oklahoma, has been active in promoting checks and balances and an independent Congress. In *Reclaiming Conservatism* (2008), he criticizes Republicans after 9/11 for "failing to scrutinize President Bush's determination to go to war in Iraq." Decisions of war, he said, "rest with the people, not an imperial 'decider-in-chief.'" Restraint of power and the division between the three branches "are at the core not only of America but of American conservatism."[46]

Defender of National Security

Over the last decade, a prominent voice promoting broad presidential powers in foreign affairs and national security is a conservative, John Yoo. Long active with the Federalist Society, he served as one of the deputies in the Office of Legal Counsel in the administration of George W. Bush. Later he returned to his position as professor of law at the University of California at Berkeley.

The framers consciously and deliberately broke with the British models of John Locke and William Blackstone, who placed all of external power and military decisions with the executive. At the Philadelphia Convention, Pierce Butler was the only delegate who wanted to vest the war power with the president, "who will have all the requisite qualities, and will not make war but when the Nation will support it."[47] Every other delegate spoke against Butler at Philadelphia and in the state ratification debates. Elbridge Gerry told his colleagues at Philadelphia that he "never expected to hear in a republic a motion to empower the Executive alone to declare war."[48]

That settled consensus was challenged by John Yoo in a lengthy article in the *California Law Review* in 1996. Relying on English history, he concluded that "the Framers created a framework designed to encourage presidential initiatives in war." Congress was given a role in war-making decisions, he argued, but not because of its authority to declare war. Legislative constraints came from powers over funding and impeachment. To Yoo, the Declare War Clause did not give Congress the power to initiate war. Instead, its purpose was to announce to other nations that America was at war, even if started by the president. In Yoo's words: "A declaration did not create or authorize; it recognized." The clause did not "add to Congress' store of war powers at the expense of the President." Rather, it gave Congress "a judicial role in declaring that a state of war exists between the United States and another nation."[49] In matters of war, Yoo wrote, federal courts "were to have no role at all."

Most law reviews are not peer-edited by experts. Second- and third-year students look for manuscripts that present original themes, are likely to stimulate debate, and be cited by other authorities and the courts. Yoo's article met those standards. In its published form it ran 139 pages and contained 625 footnotes. Even if student editors are no match for the intellectual depth and experience of authors who submit articles for consideration, it should have been within the capacity of students at the *California Law Review* to ask Yoo four fundamental questions.

First, if the framers created a constitution to encourage presidents to initiate war, why is the Constitution written the way it is? All of Blackstone's foreign policy prerogatives are vested either solely in Congress by Article I or shared between the president and the Senate. Not one of those prerogatives appears in Article II exclusively for the president. The president is commander in chief, but only one delegate (Pierce Butler) thought that the president could be safely entrusted to initiate war.

Second, if the constitutional design is intended to encourage presidents to initiate war, why did such prominent framers as John Jay, James Madison, and James Wilson consistently warn about the dangers of executive wars? Why did they assure voters in the ratification debates that the Constitution took the power of war away from the executive and placed it safely in Congress, the people's branch? Those framers viewed that constitutional principle as crucial and fundamental.

Third, if the Constitution authorizes presidents to initiate wars against other countries, why did every president from George Washington to Franklin D. Roosevelt, who decided it was necessary to engage in offensive war, come to Congress to request either a legislative declaration or authorization? No president before Truman ever claimed he could unilaterally take the country to war. Even President James Polk, having placed American soldiers in a disputed region near the Mexican border, did not believe he had the right to go to war on his own. After hostilities broke out he said that "war exists" but nevertheless came to Congress to request a declaration. Polk and Congress understood that the legislative branch needed to exercise an independent decision to authorize war, not merely bless a president's initiative.

Fourth, if courts have "no role" in questions of war, why did the Supreme Court decide such war power cases as *Bas v. Tingy* (1800), *Talbot v. Seeman* (1801), and *Little v. Barreme* (1804)? The students at the law review might have even found *United States v. Smith* (1806), a war power case decided by a federal circuit court.[50] In all of those cases the courts looked not to the president for deciding war power issues but to Congress alone. From 1789 to 1950 all three branches understood that offensive wars against other countries could be authorized solely by Congress.[51]

The scope and authority of the war power will be examined more closely in Chapter 5. Here it is sufficient to recall the congressional debate in 1917 to declare war against Germany. President Woodrow Wilson had promised in the election of 1916 to "keep the country out of war." Once returned to the White House, he decided it was time to join the bloody conflagration that became known as World War I. There was no claim on his part that the decision was his alone. He knew he had to come to Congress for statutory authority. For some members of Congress it was enough that the president had made his move and it was their duty to stand with him. Lawmakers exhausted every stale phrase possible to defend a declaration of war, including "wherever the flag leads we must follow," "America first," and the "command is 'Forward!'" Another shallow argument frequently repeated: "Stand by the president." Representative Ernest Lundeen, Republican from Minnesota, took dead aim at that platitude:

There are those who insist on the slogan, "Stand by the President." Stand by the President! Which one—the one that "kept us out of war" or the one that plunged us in? You might as well say, "Stand by Congress." Its duties are just as important and its rights just as sacred as those of the Chief Executive. A better slogan would be, Stand by the Government. . . . But why not have a still better and a still greater slogan and sentiment that comes out of the great American heart: Stand by the people. . . . I refuse to crown the President with kingly powers. I am standing by Congress in the performance of its constitutional duties. The mandate of the people is the only command I recognize, and no one can swerve me from that position.[52]

Today, both conservative and liberal scholars are busy rethinking presidential power. The halo has been removed somewhat and in its place is a more realistic attitude about the capacities of those who sit in the Oval Office. One of the curious patterns is the extent to which presidential scholars over the years have developed elaborate theories and models of an informed, responsible, and enlightened president, and how those models have scant bearing on those elected as president. From Truman to the present, occupants of the White House fall far short of the glamorous and idealized models fashioned by scholars and widely accepted by the voters.

Who Represents the National Interest?

One healthy step would be to discard the facile doctrine that associates the president with the "national interest" and lawmakers with "local" or "special interests." There is nothing automatically negative about local or special interests and certainly nothing automatically virtuous about the national interest. Every nation has a right to preserve its sovereignty and fight off invaders. There is a national interest in preserving and protecting the Constitution. There is a national interest for each branch to check each other. It is in the country's interest to have citizens criticize government, both for reasons of free speech and to limit the damage that government can do, especially in times of emergency.

It is not in the national interest to pass sedition laws, although advocates of such bills defend them precisely for that reason. The country and the Constitution are weakened by sending men and women to prison for speaking their minds. It is not in the national interest to have lawmakers spend so much time raising money for their reelection, time needed to devote to their constitutional and institutional duties. It was not in the national interest for the United States to intervene in Vietnam, even if President Johnson said it was. In his private moments he and his advisers knew it was foolhardy to commit troops to Southeast Asia. He escalated the war in Vietnam for personal and partisan reasons, not for the national interest.[53]

The Soviet Union considered it was in their national interest to spread world communism. To promote that cause, individual rights had to be suppressed. Nazi Germany concluded it was in their national interest to occupy the Sudetenland, Austria, Czechoslovakia, Poland, and the rest of Europe. Individual rights had to be subordinated to pursue this collective effort. If the national interest dominates, minorities and the politics of pluralism have no freedom to operate. The state will always trump the individual.

The perils of promoting the "national interest" have been well described by J. David Singer, who referred to it as "a smokescreen by which we all too often oversimplify the world, denigrate our rivals, enthrall our citizens, and justify acts of dubious morality and efficacy." The overriding danger is that when presidents or politicians invoke the national interest, the general public will "snap to attention, do their duty and turn off their ethical and intellectual equipment."[54] A republican form of government depends on individuals (and members of Congress) willing to exercise independent judgment.

On April 15, 1834, President Andrew Jackson in his protest of the Senate's vote to censure him described the president as "the direct representative of the American people." Presidents have a representative function, but they are elected by a portion of the country. Because of third parties, they often take office with less than 50 percent of the popular vote. Generally they have a narrow margin over defeated candidates. Members of Congress represent smaller territories, but to pass a bill these local and state interests must form a consensus. Why shouldn't the final product represent the national interest as well as, or better than, a president's proposal? Moreover, what emerges from the legislative branch reflects the agreement of *elected* officials. Other than the president and the vice president, the executive branch consists of careerists and political appointees.

Presidents cannot govern effectively by focusing exclusively on the national interest. To prevail, they necessarily seek the support of local, special, and sectional interests. Satisfying special interests can be in the national interest. Otherwise, we would never have congressionally funded bridges, roads, reclamation projects, housing assistance, government buildings, disaster relief, Pell education grants, food stamps, child nutrition, and much else that is regularly included in the federal budget.

Reconsidering Presidential Power

Presidents have injured themselves, their parties, and the country by embarking on policies claimed to be in the national interest. What is announced as national interest is often a broad cloak that conceals personal and party interests. In the 1980s, Larry Berman published a number of probing works on the miscalculations of President Lyndon Johnson in widening the Vietnam War. Using declassified documents Berman spotlighted deliberate manipulations and the steady reliance on illusions that eventually discredited Johnson, his senior advisers, and the Democratic Party. Berman's books include *Planning a Tragedy: The Americanization of the War in Vietnam* (1982) and *Lyndon Johnson's War: The Road to Stalemate in Vietnam* (1989). John Burke and Fred Greenstein, in *How Presidents Test Reality: Decisions on Vietnam, 1954 and 1965*

(1989), explained how Johnson's style of leadership (compared unfavorably with Eisenhower's) undermined the reality, feasibility, and constitutionality of U.S. national security policy.

H. R. McMaster, an air force major, published *Dereliction of Duty: Lyndon Johnson, Robert McNamara, the Joint Chiefs of Staff, and the Lies That Led to Vietnam* (1998), a scathing attack on the decisions that precipitated failures in Vietnam. In biting prose he captures Johnson's partisan calculations, poor judgments by Secretary of Defense McNamara, the timidity of the joint chiefs for failing to offer realistic options, the arrogance of Pentagon planners, and a persistent record of stealth and deception by executive officials.

Political scientist George Edwards, in an article published in 1991, described the broad constitutional role for Congress in matters of war: "There is little question that the Constitution allocates to Congress a central role in determining the major elements of national security policy if Congress chooses to do so."[55] He sharply questioned the conventional models that assigned to the president and executive officials a decided superiority in providing competent, coherent, and rational policy analysis. He found little evidence that the executive branch possessed any monopoly on wisdom that could not benefit from the regular deliberative process offered by Congress.

The University Press of Kansas regularly publishes books that analyze the importance of congressional and judicial checks on presidential military decisions. In *The Constitution and the Conduct of American Foreign Policy* (1996), David Gray Adler and Larry George edited a collection of 14 articles that looked in depth at interbranch relations in formulating national security policy. Six years later, in *The Presidency and the Law: The Clinton Legacy*, Adler teamed with Michael Genovese to explore the legal and constitutional controversies of President Bill Clinton.

Alexander DeConde, in *Presidential Machismo* (2000), released a trenchant analysis of the costs of presidential wars. He noted that presidential scholars had given the office "fictitious qualities that defied reality." He found no substantial body of evidence that in matters of war "one man can decide better than many or that the presidency ennobles the incumbent." The great danger to constitutional government, he advised, "lurks in executive machismo in the conduct of foreign affairs because it breeds contempt for law, can subvert democratic institutions, and could lead to tyranny."[56]

In an article published in 2002, Richard Pious urged a reconsideration of Neustadt's formulations, such as his distinction between the amateur (Eisenhower) who thinks first of the public interest and then of the political stakes, compared to the professional (Franklin Roosevelt) who defines the public interest in terms of his political advantage. Pious noted that the distinctions by Neustadt "have been at the core of our theoretical understanding of presidential power, but they cannot account for the spectacular failures of presidents such as Nixon, Johnson, or Clinton, all of whom understood and acted on their power stakes and showed no signs of being willing to sacrifice their political interests for any abstract conceptions of the public interest."[57]

That essay, enriched by other research, led to Pious's book *Why Presidents Fail* (2008). He explains why the neglect of law and constitutional boundaries increases the risk of presidential error. That danger expands with confidential and covert operations: "When policies are inverted and operations privatized, they attract lowlifes as middlemen and brokers, as in the Iran-Contra arms sales." A president's effort to hide his involvement adds to the risk, "because inexperienced, overly eager, or unstable operatives are recruited to do the work. They may go off the deep end or decide they have been poorly treated and betray their handlers." Blackmail, Pious warns, "is always a possibility, because if these operatives are ever caught in any illegality, their ace in the hole is to give up their White House sponsors."[58]

Pious punctures the belief that presidents enjoy a unique advantage over Congress in terms of expertise and reliable information. Despite the presence of tens of thousands of experts within executive agencies, presidents are regularly unable to obtain accurate or even semiaccurate projections about the economy, the national budget, and the military strengths or weaknesses of other nations. Administrations have failed to predict missile gaps, the collapse of the Soviet Union, and weapons of mass destruction in Iraq. The ill-conceived military initiatives with the Bay of Pigs and the war in Vietnam inflicted great damage on the country. Presidential actions with U-2 flights (Eisenhower), the Cuban Missile Crisis (Kennedy), and rescuing the American merchant ship *Mayaguez* (Ford) were all accompanied by false and deceptive executive announcements.

James P. Pfiffner and Eric Alterman have turned our attention to presidential lies, big and small.[59] In recent years, scholars have published a number of works sharply criticizing presidential claims of power and urging a return to a constitutional system of checks and balances.[60] It is too early to tell if these studies mark a permanent appreciation for constitutional values and the rule of law or whether they were largely triggered by the excesses and abuses that emerged during the administration of George W. Bush. One test will come with the Obama administration. Will the United States once again fall prey to romances about a personal presidency and ignore the structural safeguards intended by the framers?

Those who teach, write for newspapers, and opine on television can help educate the public that strong presidents are not always good presidents, there is nothing automatically superior about the "national interest," executive decisiveness is not the same as sound judgment, unleashing military might can weaken national security, and opposition to misguided and illegal presidential action is the highest form of patriotism. All of those lessons underscore the need for a strong and independent Congress to check presidential power.

CHAPTER THREE
INTERPRETING THE CONSTITUTION

From elementary school to law school to graduate school, students are likely to be taught that the U.S. Supreme Court is the dominant and final voice on the meaning of the Constitution. How did we go from popular sovereignty, with Congress as the first branch, to a system of government that places such vast power in the hands of nine justices? More precisely: in the hands of five justices who form the majority? When, why, and how was self-government shoved aside by a small elite of non-elected judges? Justice Robert Jackson offered this claim in *Brown v. Allen* (1953): "We are not final because we are infallible, but we are infallible only because we are final."[1] No one even vaguely familiar with American history could believe that the Court has been either infallible or final.

This chapter explains that judicial supremacy was never the framers' intent or aspiration. For most of its career, the Supreme Court understood that it shared constitutional interpretation with the other two federal branches, the independent states, and the general public. Only in the last half-century has the Court pretended to be the Final Word. That claim is regularly exploded when one follows how judicial rulings are actually implemented. Congress has always played a significant role in constitutional interpretation, often substituting its judgment for the rulings of courts.

The Misunderstood *Marbury* Case

Judicial review is the power of courts to declare the acts of other branches and the states unconstitutional. Although not expressly provided for in the Constitution, judicial review is implied at least in a limited sense. Were Congress to reduce the salaries of federal courts, judges would properly strike down the legislation as a violation of express language in Article III: Federal judges shall receive a compensation "which shall not be diminished during their Continuance in Office." As with other branches, the judiciary has every right to protect its independence and fight off encroachments. The Constitution states that Congress shall not pass a "bill of attainder" (legislative punishment without trial). Were Congress to use its appropriations power to deny salaries to executive officials because of their political views and opinions, the Supreme Court would be justified in nullifying the statutory language, as it did in *United States v. Lovett* (1946).[2]

Beyond clear cases grounded in constitutional text lies a much larger universe of complex questions presented to the Court. If the lawsuit is a "case or controversy," the Court has jurisdiction to hear the dispute and decide it. Does the Court's ruling then become binding, conclusive, and irreversible? Or may other branches, the 50 states, and the general public reenter the field and participate again, leading to a different result? The history of the United States is very much the latter.

Judicial review dates from the famous case of *Marbury v. Madison* (1803).[3] Before that decision, justices were uncertain whether they had authority to strike down the actions of Congress or the executive branch. In *Hylton v. United States* (1796), the Court upheld a congressional statute that imposed a tax on carriages. If justices had authority to uphold a statute, did that mean they could invalidate one? Apparently so. In *Hylton*, Justice

Samuel Chase tiptoed around the question, saying it was unnec-essary "*at this time*, for me to determine, whether this court, *con-stitutionally* possesses the power to declare an act of Congress void.... [B]ut if the court have such power, I am free to declare, that I will never exercise it, *but in a very clear case*."[4]

Two years later, in *Hollingsworth v. Virginia*, the Court upheld the process Congress used for constitutional amend-ments.[5] In a case also decided in 1798, *Calder v. Bull*, Justice James Iredell echoed the sentiments of Justice Chase. If a statute passed by Congress or one of the states violated the express con-stitutional provision on ex post facto laws, "it is unquestionably void; though, I admit, that as the authority to declare it void is of delicate and awful nature, the Court will never resort to that authority, but in a clear and urgent case."[6]

In *Marbury v. Madison*, the Court for the first time invalidat-ed a section of a congressional statute. That decision is regularly cited by justices today to defend the proposition that the judici-ary is supreme and final on fixing the meaning of the Constitu-tion. Such an interpretation was never on the mind of the author of *Marbury*, Chief Justice John Marshall. The Court in 1803 was in far too weak a position, politically and institution-ally, to claim supremacy over the other two branches. The Jeffer-sonians had taken control of the White House and both chambers of Congress. Muscle-flexing by the Court would have been disastrous for the judiciary, the one branch the Federalist Party still controlled.

Here was Marshall's predicament. William Marbury and several other individuals had received judicial appointments during the final days of the administration of John Adams. Some of the commissions were not delivered. Marbury took his case directly to the Supreme Court, asking that it exercise its power under Section 13 of the Judiciary Act of 1789 and issue a writ of mandamus, compelling Secretary of State James Madi-son to deliver his commission. Marshall knew that any order he issued would be ignored by Madison and President Jefferson. Marshall saw no point in provoking a confrontation he could not possibly win. Instead, he ruled that the mandamus provision was unconstitutional. His reasoning (distinguishing between appellate and original jurisdiction) was not very persuasive but it saved the Court from a humiliating defeat. There was nothing in Marshall's decision to imply judicial superiority over constitutional interpretation.

Take a look at the sentence in *Marbury* that is regularly cited to defend judiciary supremacy: "It is emphatically the province and duty of the judicial department to say what the law is."[7] Read that language with care. It contains nothing about judiciary supremacy. It says that courts decide cases, which is of course true. That is why we have courts. But it would be just as true to write: "It is emphatically the province and duty of the legislative department to say what the law is." No one could disagree with that sentence, and yet it would be misleading to claim that Congress held final authority to say what the law is. Presidents may exercise their veto power and courts can review congressional statutes both for meaning and constitutionality. All three branches are deeply involved in deciding what the law is. So are the 50 states, jurors, and citizens at large. Examples of this rich and ongoing constitutional dialogue are provided in this chapter and the next.

John Marshall had another reason not to claim that the Court was superior to the other branches. He decided *Marbury* on February 24, 1803. The House impeached District Judge John Pickering on March 2, 1803, and the Senate removed him on March 12, 1804. The House then impeached Justice Samuel Chase, in large part for his partisan conduct toward opponents of the John Adams administration. Had he been removed by the Senate, the House might have next turned the impeachment machinery against Marshall. It was in this tense political climate that Marshall wrote to Chase on January 23, 1805, offering private views about the legislative threat. Marshall advised that if Congress disliked a judicial opinion it could simply pass legislation to reverse the ruling. There was no need to impeach judges. Far from boasting about judiciary supremacy, Marshall referred to the "mildness of our character." Here is what Marshall wrote to Chase: "I think the modern doctrine of impeachment should yield to an appellate jurisdiction in the legislature. A reversal of those legal opinions deemed unsound by the legislature would certainly better comport with the mildness of our character than [would] a removal of the judge who has rendered them unknowing of his fault."[8]

Judges and scholars who treat *Marbury* as the source of judicial supremacy ignore what happened during Marshall's tenure from 1801 to 1835. *Marbury* was the one and only time that Marshall invalidated a statute passed by Congress. He used judicial review primarily to *uphold* congressional power and federal regulation over the states. He consistently found ways to support legislation that Congress passed to create the U.S. Bank and exercise the commerce power. Judicial review was not wielded as a nay-saying axe against Congress—against state action on occasion, yes, but not against the coequal national branches. Judicial review was used affirmatively to justify and legitimate what they decided to do. Members of Congress took the lead in determining how they could exercise their express and implied powers. The Court then sanctioned the legislative judgment.

Early Constitutional Disputes

In the early decades, Congress and the president necessarily made independent judgments about the meaning of the Constitution. Few decisions of the Supreme Court or the lower courts provided much guidance on these issues. The two elected branches debated and reached agreement on the constitutionality of the U.S. Bank, the congressional investigative power, the president's power to remove top executive officials, the principle of federalism, internal improvements, the war-making power, treaties and foreign relations, and the scope of the commerce power. It was in the elected branches, "not in the courts, that the original understanding of the Constitution was forged."[9]

Private citizens also helped determine what was constitutional. In 1793, President George Washington issued what has come to be known as the Neutrality Proclamation. He directed Americans not to take sides in the war between England and France. Individuals who defied the proclamation were prosecuted. However, the constitutionality of the proclamation was not decided in the courts by federal judges. Ordinary citizens, serving as jurors, put a check on Washington. They advised federal prosecutors that proclamations issued by British kings might have been treated as law, but in America the only way to create criminal law was action by Congress by statute. The message from jurors was clear: If you bring a prosecution based solely on the proclamation we will acquit. President Washington heard the communication clearly and came to Congress to seek legislation. The result was the Neutrality Act of 1794, providing legal authority to prosecute and punish individuals who violated federal law.[10] Jurors sitting on trials directed the administration to respect and follow the principles of self-government.

Another constitutional issue decided largely outside the courts was whether the government could punish citizens for what they said or wrote. At times prosecution was based on a statute, such as the Sedition Act of 1798, discussed in the first chapter. Another option was the doctrine of "seditious libel," drawn from British common law. Once in power, the Jeffersonians were willing to use seditious libel to punish Federalist newspapers that criticized the administration. Many of these cases were brought at the state level. The case that reached the Supreme Court in 1812 was a federal, not a state, case. The individuals prosecuted were editors of a Federalist newspaper in Connecticut. The Court noted that it was the first time that it had been faced with the question whether federal courts had jurisdiction over seditious libel. It concluded that the issue had "been long since settled in public opinion." It meant that Congress had yet to establish by law that criticism of the national government was a criminal act. In short, constitutional law was decided by the people, working through their representatives, not by the courts. Whatever the law in England, the exercise of criminal jurisdiction in common law cases was not within the implied powers of federal courts.[11]

The Supreme Court learned that its decisions were anything but final. During the 1850s, the Court held that the height of a bridge over the Ohio River, constructed under state law, was a "nuisance" because it obstructed navigation. Congress passed a law a few months later declaring that bridge and a second one to be "lawful structures." Which branch should be supreme on this question? The Court had first held the bridge was to be illegal. Now, because of congressional action, it decided the structures were legal. Three justices, writing in dissent, were dumbfounded. They thought that when the Court initially held the bridge to be obstructive, that was the end of the matter. How could Congress come along and reach an opposite judgment? What did this do to the finality of judicial decisions or the dignity of the Court? Their objections have remained very much a minority position. The Court frequently acknowledges in this type of case on state power that if Congress by statute contradicts a Court opinion, the Court will acquiesce to the legislative judgment.[12]

In the decades leading up to the Civil War, the political engine for eliminating slavery came not from the three branches of government but from private citizens. Large numbers of Americans, regarding slavery as a violation of the principles stated in the Declaration of Independence, pressed for abolition. "All men are created equal" left no room for slavery. Americans during that period "were not inclined to leave to private lawyers any more than to public men the conception, execution, and interpretation of public law. The conviction was general that no aristocracy existed with respect to the Constitution. Like politics, with which it was inextricably joined, the Constitution was everyone's business."[13]

By the time the slavery issue reached the national government in the late 1850s, all three branches had failed in their public duties. President James Buchanan, who wanted to mention slavery in his inaugural address in March 1857, learned from several justices that the Supreme Court was about to decide the pending case of *Dred Scott v. Sandford*.[14] Buchanan proceeded to tell the country that the controversy over slavery was "a judicial question, which legitimately belongs to the Supreme Court of the United States, before whom it is now pending, and will, it is understood, be speedily and finally settled. To their decision, in common with all good citizens, I shall cheerfully submit, whatever this may be, . . ." He might have been willing to defer to the Court; the country did not.

In *Dred Scott*, the Court held that the "enslaved African race" could not be citizens of the United States and could not sue in federal court. It also ruled that Congress lacked authority to prevent the spread of slavery to the territories in the West and that therefore the Missouri Compromise statute was unconstitutional. Newspapers differed in their views about the "finality" of this decision. To the *New York Tribune* the Court's action "we need hardly say, is entitled to just as much moral weight as would be the judgment of a majority of those congregated in any Washington bar-room."[15] Newspapers in the South joined with President Buchanan in accepting the ruling as the final word.

During the campaign of 1858, Senator Stephen Douglas treated *Dred Scott* as conclusive and binding. His opponent, Abraham Lincoln, accepted the decision only to the extent that it affected the particular litigants. He refused to accept the decision as national policy.[16] In his first inaugural address, Lincoln explained the conditions under which a decision of the Court is binding:

> I do not forget the position assumed by some that constitutional questions are to be decided by the Supreme Court, nor do I deny that such decisions must be binding in any case upon the parties to a suit as to the object of that suit, while they are also entitled to a very high respect and consideration in all parallel cases by all other departments of the Government. . . . At the same time, the candid citizen must confess that if the policy of the Government upon vital questions affecting the whole people is to be irrevoca-

bly fixed by decisions of the Supreme Court, the instant they are made in ordinary litigation between parties in personal actions the people will have ceased to be their own rulers, having to that extent practically resigned their Government into the hands of that eminent tribunal.

On November 29, 1862, Attorney General Edward Bates released a legal opinion that repudiated the reasoning of *Dred Scott*. He concluded that men of color, if born in the United States, are citizens of the United States. The rest of the Court's decision was rejected in 1862 when Congress passed legislation prohibiting slavery in the territories. During legislative debate, no member of Congress even referred to the Court's decision or felt in any way bound by it. Lawmakers decided they were free to exercise independent judgment on the constitutional issue, with or without the Court. The Thirteenth Amendment, adopted in 1865, abolished the institution of slavery. The Fourteenth Amendment, ratified in 1868, provided for the equality of blacks before the law. It specifically provides that all persons born in the United States are American citizens and of the state in which they reside. The Fifteenth Amendment, which became effective in 1870, gave blacks the right to vote. In other areas of public policy, Congress would continue to press its understanding of the Constitution in the face of contrary positions by the Court.

Efforts to Regulate the Economy

Many of the constitutional disputes after the Civil War, pitting Congress against the Supreme Court, involved economic issues of federal currency, taxation, and government regulation. Judicial decisions at times blocked congressional legislation but only temporarily. Either by a change in membership on the Court, constitutional amendments, or subsequent statutory action, Congress regularly prevailed. The dominant branch in these struggles was Congress, not the judiciary. The Court conceded in 1946: "The history of judicial limitation of congressional power over commerce, when exercised affirmatively, has been more largely one of retreat than of ultimate victory."[17] In 1951, Justice Owen Roberts reached a similar conclusion: "Looking back, it is difficult to see how the Court could have resisted the popular urge for uniform standards throughout the country— for what in effect was a unified economy."[18] Justice Robert Jackson observed in a 1951 speech: "The practical play of the forces of politics is such that judicial power has often delayed but never permanently defeated the persistent will of a substantial majority."[19]

An early collision between Congress and the Court after the Civil War involved the issue of "greenbacks." When President Lincoln entered the White House in March 1861 he discovered that the U.S. Treasury had hardly any money and little in the way of precious metals (gold and silver) to support money that circulated as legal tender. On February 25, 1862, Congress enacted a bill that authorized the issuance of paper notes to be accepted as legal tender to pay debts and other obligations. The notes, printed on one side in black and green, became known as "greenbacks." There was no dispute about the legality of the bills for present and future use, but were they legal to settle prior debts?

That question reached the Supreme Court in *Hepburn v. Griswold* (1870).[20] At that time, the Court consisted of eight justices. A narrow majority of 4 to 3 decided that the statute was unconstitutional because debts entered into before passage of the law had to be repaid in gold and silver. In earlier decisions, from 1863 to 1869, 15 state courts of last resort had upheld the Legal Tender Act of 1862. One court, from Kentucky, found the statute unconstitutional, and it was that case that reached the Supreme Court in *Hepburn v. Griswold*. Initially it looked like the eight justices on the Court were equally divided, but Justice Robert Grier switched his vote and the majority seemed to be five to three against the statute.

Changing votes did much to discredit the Court. It planned to issue a decision on January 31, 1870, one day before Grier's resignation. However, Justice Samuel Miller asked for an additional week to finish his dissenting opinion, delaying the release of the opinion until February 7. By that time Grier had resigned, putting the majority at four to three. There was little reason to think that the slim majority would survive. President Ulysses S. Grant appointed two new justices, one to replace Grier and a second to fill a new position created by Congress.

The two nominees, William Strong of Pennsylvania and Joseph P. Bradley of New Jersey, appeared likely to uphold the Legal Tender Act. Strong, as a member of the Pennsylvania Supreme Court, had already upheld the statute, and Bradley seemed likely to vote the same way. In the *Legal Tender Cases* (1871), the Court five to four reversed *Hepburn v. Griswold* and ruled that the statute of 1862 was constitutional.[21] The one-year turnaround highlighted that the meaning of the Constitution does not depend on fixed and eternal principles discovered by the judiciary but rather in no small part on the Court's membership and new appointments.

Over the years, federal courts tried to carve out exclusive jurisdictions for the national government and the states. The Supreme Court remarked in *United States v. Cruikshank* (1876): "The powers which one possesses, the other does not."[22] But national and state powers were not that precise, especially in the field of commerce. In *Leisy v. Hardin* (1890), the Court held that the power of Congress over interstate commerce trumped state powers and local options.[23] If a state prohibited intoxicating liquors from entering its territory, the prohibition could not apply to incoming original packages or kegs. The state could regulate the material only after the original packages had been broken into smaller units. In so deciding, the Court added an important qualifier: States could not exclude the incoming articles "without congressional permission."

The constitutional meaning of interstate commerce therefore depended on what members of Congress decided to do. Less than a month after the Court's decision, Congress began debate on legislation to give the states independent authority to regulate incoming liquor. The determination of lawmakers to exercise independent judgment is reflected in comments from Senator George Edmunds of Vermont. He said the opinions of the Court regarding Congress "are of no more value to us than ours are to it. We are just as independent of the Supreme Court of the United States as it is of us, and every judge will admit it." If members of Congress concluded that the Court had made an error, "are we to stop and say that is the end of the law and the mission of civilization in the United States for that reason? I take it not." Further deliberation by the Court might produce a different result: "[A]s they have often done, it may be their mission next year to change their opinion and say that the rule ought to be the other way."[24]

The decision in *Leisy* is dated April 28, 1890. Less than four months later, on August 8, Congress enacted legislation overriding the Court. The law provided that all fermented, distilled, or other intoxicating liquors or liquids transported into any state or territory for use, consumption, or sale "shall upon arrival in such State or Territory be subject to the operation and effect of the laws of such State or Territory enacted in the exercise of its police powers to the same extent and in the same manner as though such liquids or liquors had been produced in such State or Territory, and shall not be exempt therefrom by reason of being introduced in original packages or otherwise." A year later, in a ruling called *In re Rahrer* (1891), the Court decided that Congress was authorized to act as it did.[25]

National debate over a federal income tax produced a pitched battle between Congress and the Court that had to be resolved by a constitutional amendment. The Court's performance damaged its prestige. The Constitution speaks clearly only about one aspect of the taxing power: "No Tax or Duty shall be laid on Articles exported from any State" (Article I, Section 9). The Constitution refers to "direct taxes" and "indirect taxes" and requires the latter to adhere to the rule of uniformity: "The Congress shall have Power to lay and collect Taxes, Duties, Imposts, and Excises, to pay the Debts and provide for the common Defence and general Welfare of the United States; but all

Duties, Imposts and Excises shall be uniform throughout the United States" (Article I, Section 8). The purpose of this language is to protect states from discriminatory actions by the national government.

The problem is that there was no clear understanding about direct taxes. The Constitution states: "No Capitation, or other direct, Tax shall be laid, unless in Proportion to the Census or Enumeration herein before directed to be taken." Congress has never relied on capitation taxes or "head taxes," which would levy a fixed rate on each person regardless of income or worth. Must all other direct taxes be levied among the states in accordance with the rule of apportionment? The Court's decision in *Hylton v. United States* (1796), involving a carriage tax, provided some guidance for constitutional analysis.[26] Further direction came from a congressional enactment in 1861 for a direct tax of $20,000,000 to be apportioned among the states. The same statute included an income tax of 3 percent for those whose annual income exceeded $800. That tax was not apportioned among the states. A decision by the Court in *Veazie Bank v. Fenno* (1869) supplied additional clues.[27] The Court, holding that a federal tax on circulation bank notes was not a direct tax, drew attention to the debates at the 1787 Philadelphia Constitutional Convention. When Massachusetts delegate Rufus King asked his colleagues for the meaning of direct taxation, "no one answered."

In *Springer v. United States* (1881), a unanimous Court decided that direct taxes meant capitation taxes and taxes on real estate.[28] To the Court, a federal income tax enacted in 1864 and amended the next year was an indirect tax. To the extent the tax inflicted "any wrong or unnecessary harshness, it was for Congress, or the people who make congresses, to see that the evil was corrected. The remedy does not lie with the judicial branch of the government."[29] Here the Court appeared to come down strongly on the side of popular sovereignty and the capacity of Congress to determine for itself the meaning of the Constitution. As with *Veazie*, the Court pointed to the debates at the

Philadelphia Convention to underscore the vague meaning of "direct taxes." After reviewing tax laws from 1789 to 1861, the Court concluded that whenever the federal government imposed a direct tax it was only on real estate and slaves. How would those precedents bear on the constitutionality of a federal income tax?

In 1894, Congress enacted a tax on individual and corporate incomes, to be effective January 1, 1895. The constitutional issue was taken quickly to the Supreme Court, which decided in *Pollock v. Farmers' Loan & Trust Co.* (1895) that the tax on rents or income from real estate was a direct tax and violated the Constitution by not adhering to the apportionment rule.[30] A second decision, under the same case name, struck down the income tax. Flavoring the decision and the legal analysis were fears of socialism and communism. During oral argument in the first case, private attorney Joseph H. Choate warned the Court that the income tax was "communistic in its purposes and tendencies."[31] Writing as part of the majority in this case, Justice Stephen Field predicted that the "present assault upon capital is but the beginning," leading to "a war of the poor against the rich; a war constantly growing in intensity and bitterness."[32]

The second decision was subject to special criticism. The Court split five to four, and one justice evidently switched sides. When the question of the income tax was addressed in the first case, the justices divided four to four. Not participating in that case was Justice Howell Jackson, but in the second case he voted to *uphold* the income tax. That should have produced a majority of five justices in support of the federal income tax, yet it went the other way. Someone changed his position. Exactly which justice moved over has never been revealed. Because of the narrow five-to-four majority and the vote switch, this decision has been called one of three "self-inflicted wounds" on the Court, the other two being *Dred Scott* and the *Legal Tender Cases*.[33]

Each chamber of Congress passed a resolution to set in motion an amendment to the Constitution to authorize a federal income tax. The Sixteenth Amendment, ratified in 1913, provides: "The Congress shall have power to lay and collect taxes on incomes, from whatever source derived, without apportionment among the several States, and without regard to any census or enumeration."

Regulating Child Labor

An especially bitter and protracted legislative-judicial clash involved efforts by the national government to place statutory constraints on child labor. Repeatedly the Supreme Court struck down congressional initiatives to regulate this area. At first lawmakers relied on the Commerce Clause and later turned to the taxing power. Blocked each time by the Court, Congress passed a constitutional amendment but could not attract sufficient states to have it ratified. Eventually the composition of the Court changed to assure not only judicial acceptance of the legislative judgment but validation by a unanimous opinion.

In 1916, Congress passed legislation to prevent the products of child labor from being shipped interstate. The legislative history explained the dangers facing young workers under age 16 in hazardous and burdensome occupations, including factories, mines, and quarries. Some children worked 11-hour days 6 days a week. Children as young as 12 worked 11 hours a day. Congress concluded that it had ample constitutional authority under the Commerce Clause to regulate public health and morals. The Supreme Court disagreed. A five-to-four majority in *Hammer v. Dagenhart* (1918) struck down the law as beyond the scope of the commerce power and an invasion of powers reserved to the states.[34] The Court reasoned that although child labor might have harmful effects on the children employed, the "goods shipped are of themselves harmless." Whatever might be necessary to regulate child labor, said the Court, had to be left to the states operating under their police powers.

Members of Congress refused to accept the Court's ruling as the last word on regulating child labor. To them, the superior body to decide national policy was Congress, not the judiciary. During debate on a bill to replace the one the Court declared invalid, Senator Robert Owen of Oklahoma rejected the argument that federal judges are somehow better able to interpret the Constitution than members of Congress:

> It is said by some that the judges are much more learned and wiser than Congress in construing the Constitution. I can not concede to this whimsical notion. They are not more learned; they are not wiser; they are not more patriotic; and what is the fatal weakness if they make their mistakes there is no adequate means of correcting their judicial errors, while if Congress should err the people have an immediate redress; they can change the House of Representatives almost immediately and can change two-thirds of the Senate within four years, while the judges are appointed for life and are removable only by impeachment.[35]

A new child labor bill enacted in 1919 rested wholly on the taxing power. The bill imposed an excise tax of 10 percent on any company operating a mine, quarry, mill, cannery, workshop, or factory that employed children of certain ages working at hours prohibited by Congress. Some lawmakers, reluctant to use the power of the national government to regulate the states, made an exception to deal with what they considered to be the evils of child labor. After a lower court ruled the statute invalid, the matter came once again to the Supreme Court.

In defending the authority of Congress to regulate child labor, Solicitor General James Beck urged the Court to respect the judgment of the people and their representatives to decide national policy. During oral argument, he warned that any action by the judiciary to invalidate the child labor law would weaken public support and acceptance of the Constitution. The "erroneous" idea that the Court is the "sole guardian and protector of our constitutional form of government has inevitably led to an impairment, both with the people and with their representatives, of what may be called the constitutional conscience."[36] It was healthy in a system of popular sovereignty to have constitutional issues debated and resolved by the general public instead of shifting those questions to the courts.

In *Bailey v. Drexel Furniture Co.* (1922), the Court mounted a majority of eight to one in striking down the child labor statute.[37] The new legislative strategy did not persuade the Court, which said it would have to "be blind not to see that the so-called tax is imposed to stop the employment of children within the age limits prescribed." The prohibited and regulatory effect and purpose seemed obvious to the Court: "All others can see and understand this. How can we properly shut our minds to it?" The subject of child labor, said the Court, had to be left to the states to regulate. To permit Congress to tax child labor "would be to break down all constitutional limitation of the powers of Congress and completely wipe out the sovereignty of the States."[38]

Even with this lopsided defeat, Congress refused to accept the Court's ruling as the final word on child labor. In 1924, both chambers of Congress passed a constitutional amendment to give Congress the power to "limit, regulate and prohibit the labor of persons under 18 years of age." Twenty-eight states ultimately ratified the amendment but 36 were needed.

Tension between the judiciary and the elected branches led to a court-packing plan offered by President Franklin D. Roosevelt in 1937. It authorized the president to nominate justices to the Supreme Court whenever an incumbent over the age of 70 declined to resign or retire. Had his plan been adopted, Roosevelt could have named as many as 6 new justices. He wanted the same authority for the lower courts, opening the possibility of 50 new judgeships.

Congress rejected the plan, but the confrontation appeared to persuade some justices to be more accepting of national regulation. By 1935, the Court was already moving in a direction to accommodate federal legislation.[39] Early in 1937 Congress passed legislation to provide full judicial pay during retirement. Perhaps because of that benefit, the conservative justice Willis

Van Devanter retired on June 2, 1937, giving Roosevelt his first opportunity in more than four years to nominate someone to the Court. Other justices retired, allowing Roosevelt to nominate Felix Frankfurter, James Byrnes, William O. Douglas, Frank Murphy, Stanley Reed, and Robert Jackson. The Court was now fundamentally restructured.

In 1938, Congress attached a child labor section to the Fair Labor Standards Act. Far from acquiescing to the judicial reasoning in *Hammer v. Dagenhart*, Congress once again based its authority to regulate child labor on its commerce power. In *United States v. Darby* (1941), a reconstituted Court upheld the child labor provision. Strikingly, the vote was unanimous.[40] The Court conceded that *Dagenhart* had been repudiated over the years and that congressional regulation of child labor was not "a forbidden invasion of state power." It found the conclusion "inescapable" that *Dagenhart* "was a departure from the principles which have prevailed in the interpretation of the Commerce Clause both before and since the decision"[41] and therefore overruled *Dagenhart*. Congress and the country, going head to head against the Court in interpreting the Constitution, had prevailed.

A Judicial Option: Someone Else Do It

Many constitutional issues do not reach the courts. Even when they do, they are regularly turned aside by the judiciary and sent back to the elected branches and the general public for resolution. An example is what is called the Statement and Account Clause. Article I, Section 9, Clause 7 of the Constitution provides: "A regular Statement and Account of the Receipts and Expenditures of all public Money shall be published from time to time." It was deemed essential in republican government that citizens know how public funds are received and spent. Accountability to the people by federal representatives is a fundamental value. The language "from time to time" gave the government some discretion over the release of financial data. At the

Virginia ratifying convention in 1788, George Mason said that the words "from time to time" were added because "there might be some matters which might require secrecy."[42] He did not mean that that information could be withheld permanently. Some delay might be justified.

In 1790, Congress began to authorize a very selective and limited use of secret expenditures. It gave the president a $40,000 account to be used for foreign intercourse, reserving to the president the discretion to decide the degree to which the expenditures should be made public. He could provide public vouchers, explaining how the money was used, or resort to unvouchered expenditures. Other confidential and unvouchered accounts appeared over the years. From 1789 to 1935, Congress departed from the Statement and Account Clause on rare occasions to permit unvouchered expenditures by the president, the secretary of the navy, and the Federal Bureau of Investigation. In each case the amounts were modest: in the range of $70,000 or less.[43]

World War II provoked greater recourse to secret funding, especially the appropriation of billions of dollars to fund development of the atomic bomb (the Manhattan Project). Many agencies began to receive authority to spend money without vouchers, including the White House, the Defense Department, the District of Columbia, the attorney general, the Bureau of Narcotics and Dangerous Drugs, the Secret Service, the Coast Guard, the Bureau of Customs, and the Immigration and Naturalization Service. Typically these were for small amounts.

Far greater in magnitude are the secret expenditures of the U.S. intelligence community, consisting of the Central Intelligence Agency, the National Security Agency, the Defense Intelligence Agency, and more than a dozen other agencies. Tens of billions are spent for these purposes, creating two major problems. One is the integrity of the Statement and Account Clause, designed to protect republican government. The other is deceptive budgeting. In order to provide the intelligence community with undisclosed amounts, it is necessary to pad the appropriation accounts that are made public. To do that, members of

Congress end up voting on statutory language that is not what it appears to be.

William B. Richardson, at attorney in Pennsylvania, decided to take the constitutional issue to the courts in the 1960s. He wanted the judiciary to declare secret funding for the CIA a violation of the Statement and Account Clause. A district court held that he lacked standing to bring the lawsuit because he could not point to a sufficient injury to himself. An appellate court held that the district court lacked jurisdiction to even hear the case. The Supreme Court refused to take this case, but several years later Richardson was again in the courts, asking that the secretary of the treasury be compelled to make a public account of CIA receipts and expenditures. This time an appellate court held that he had standing and that the government had to publish the figures.

In *United States v. Richardson* (1974), the Supreme Court threw the case out on the ground of standing.[44] Divided five to four, it concluded that the subject matter of the lawsuit demanded that the issue be left "to the surveillance of Congress, and ultimately to the political process." In one of the dissents, Justice William O. Douglas objected that standing should not be invoked to read the Statement and Account Clause "out of the Constitution" when it comes to certain intelligence agencies. Such a proposition, he said, was "astounding."[45] Justices William J. Brennan, Potter Stewart, and Thurgood Marshall wrote separate dissents.

Congress held hearings on disclosing the aggregate amount of the budget for the intelligence community. I testified before the House Intelligence Committee in 1994, urging that the aggregate amount be made public, both to comply with the Statement and Account Clause and to eliminate deceptive budgeting practices. Sometimes one chamber would support disclosure, and at other times the second chamber, but never both in the same Congress. Although a presidential commission in 1996 recommended disclosure of the aggregate, no legislation resulted.

Inadvertently, the commission publicly released the budgets of the National Reconnaissance Office ($6.2 billion), the National Security Agency ($3.7 billion), the Central Intelligence Agency ($3.1 billion), and the Defense Intelligence Agency ($2 billion).[46]

Litigation in the 1990s by Steven Aftergood of the Federation of American Scientists prompted the CIA in 1997 to release the aggregate figure of $26.7 billion (of which the CIA represented $3 billion). The aggregate for the next year: $26.7 billion.[47] After that point the CIA refused to release the figures. In 2004, the 9/11 Commission recommended public disclosure of the aggregate amount. Three years later Congress passed legislation to implement the recommendation. The intelligence community released the aggregate amount of $43.5 billion for fiscal year 2007. After adding the amounts spent by the military services for intelligence operations, the total exceeds $50 billion.[48] A constitutional dispute that could not be resolved in the courts was settled through the regular political process.

Another constitutional issue involving the CIA arose in 1997. The Senate Intelligence Committee drafted legislation to authorize employees within the intelligence community to report directly to the intelligence committees when they learned of illegality, gross mismanagement, gross waste of funds, and other agency misconduct. The Justice Department regarded this type of legislation as an unconstitutional encroachment of the president's authority over the executive branch. Asked to testify before the committee in February 1998, I defended the constitutional right of Congress to gain access to disclosures by lower-level employees about agency wrongdoing. I was asked to testify a week later, this time sitting next to an attorney from the Justice Department, who continued to raise constitutional objections. Two hours after the hearing, the committee unanimously voted (19 to 0) to report the bill. I testified in favor of the legislation before the House Intelligence Committee. With some changes made to reconcile the Senate and House bills, the legislation was signed into law.[49]

The Durable Legislative Veto

In the 1800s, Congress began to use legislative vehicles short of a public law to control executive agencies. At times Congress relied on simple resolutions (passed by one chamber) and at other times adopted concurrent resolutions (passed by both chambers but not presented to the president for his signature or veto). Although those procedures lacked the force of law, agencies generally found it prudent to comply with one-house and two-house legislative vetoes.

What if this process had been sanctioned by a public law? Would they be legally binding? In 1854, Attorney General Caleb Cushing reasoned that simple resolutions could compel a department head to act if they had been recognized by a previous law.[50] By the early 1900s, Congress was using simple and concurrent resolutions to control certain operations within the executive branch, such as directing the secretary of war to investigate matters relating to rivers and harbors.

President Woodrow Wilson issued constitutional objections to legislative vetoes. In one veto message, he told Congress it could not use a concurrent resolution to remove the comptroller general and the assistant comptroller general. Congress responded by replacing the concurrent resolution with a joint resolution, which passes both chambers and is submitted to the president. Wilson also objected to a process that allowed the Joint Committee on Printing to issue regulations controlling what would be printed and what would be discontinued.

Some presidents recognized the benefit of a legislative veto. President Herbert Hoover wanted to reorganize the executive branch to save money but understood that if he submitted a bill to Congress it could either be ignored or so amended that he would not like the final product. In his first annual message to Congress in 1929, he recommended that Congress delegate reorganization powers to him, subject to some form of legislative veto, including even a committee veto. Congress would have to disapprove within a set period of time, acting up or down on his proposal without any amendments. Congress agreed to that process in 1932, reserving for itself a one-house legislative veto within 60 days. By the time Hoover submitted a reorganization plan, he had been defeated for reelection. On January 19, 1933, the House of Representatives passed a resolution disapproving all of his proposals, preferring to leave agency restructuring to his successor, Franklin D. Roosevelt.[51]

Roosevelt struggled with the merits of the legislative veto, finding it unconstitutional on some occasions but embracing it when it offered important advantages. His arguments had less to do with strict constitutional principles than with his desire for additional authority and flexibility. If he needed to swallow a legislative veto to get authority he wanted, he would do so. The record of subsequent presidents has also been inconsistent. President Dwight D. Eisenhower opposed committee vetoes in one form, yet consented to others. Over the decades, the legislative veto spread from executive reorganization to cover federal salaries, impoundment of funds, war powers, national emergencies, presidential papers, and agency regulations.

Whatever advantages presidents had found over the years, by the time of President Jimmy Carter it was decided to take a stand against all legislative vetoes. In 1978, Carter issued a major critique of the process. Nevertheless, White House aides and the Justice Department gave some ground and announced an accommodation for certain kinds of legislative vetoes, particularly over executive reorganization and war powers. Litigation produced many conflicting positions by federal courts. It appeared to some observers that the constitutionality of the legislative veto would be settled once and for all with the 1983 case of *INS v. Chadha*.[52]

With *Chadha* heading to the Supreme Court, I wrote an article predicting that the legislative veto would survive even if the justices found it unconstitutional. My work with the appropriations committees convinced me that Congress and executive agencies were satisfied with a process they had perfected over the decades. It involved "reprogramming of funds"—moving funds within an appropriations account to satisfy new needs. Once a fiscal year begins, it becomes evident that Congress and the agencies failed to anticipate certain budgetary needs. Legal and technical developments can play havoc with agency projections. For whatever reason, it was often important to shift money from a program of lesser priority to one of greater priority.

Congress was not about to leave those decisions entirely to the agencies. The two branches worked out detailed agreements on how to handle reprogramming. In some cases the agencies need only notify the committees of jurisdiction. For other reprogramming actions, the agencies would have to seek and obtain prior approval from those committees. Nothing the Supreme Court would decide about the legislative veto, at some abstract level of constitutional principle, would eliminate the effectiveness, attractiveness, and continuity of this agency-committee process.[53]

In *INS v. Chadha* (1983), the Supreme Court held the legislative veto to be unconstitutional. The procedure challenged in the lawsuit was a one-house veto over deportation decisions, but the Court swept broadly (too broadly), insisting that whenever Congress intends to control activities outside the legislative branch, it must comply with two requirements: bicameralism (action by both chambers) and presentment (submitting a bill to the president for his signature or veto). This analysis invalidated every form of legislative veto: one-house, two-house, committee, and subcommittee. The Court wrote: "the fact that a given law or procedure is efficient, convenient, and useful in facilitating functions of government, standing alone, will not save it if it is contrary to the Constitution. Convenience and efficiency are not the primary objectives—or the hallmarks—of democratic government."[54]

This lofty language masked a failure to understand how the legislative veto began and why it flourished. For the Court, the legislative veto seemed to originate from lawmakers determined to meddle in executive decisions. Yet it was President Hoover who asked for the legislative veto, and other presidents tolerated the process because it brought with it tangible benefits, including broad delegations of legislative power. At no point in the Court's decision did it attempt to analyze and comprehend the complex negotiations that allowed agencies and congressional committees to reach agreement on reprogramming actions.

Committee vetoes retained their vitality after *Chadha*. Between 1983 and 2009, the number of new legislative vetoes enacted has exceeded 1,000. Unlike earlier versions that operated in plain sight (one-house and two-house vetoes), committee and subcommittee controls over reprogramming are largely subterranean and invisible. Presidents regularly condemn these provisions when they sign bills, suggesting that agencies need only notify committees of executive decisions. But it does not work that way. Agencies in the decades after *Chadha* continue to spell out in their budget manuals the reprogramming actions that need notification and those that require prior approval. The particular committees involved in this process are identified in the budget manuals. The appropriations committees are centrally involved, but authorizing committees are frequently included. Depending on the agreement fashioned, agencies seek prior approval from a committee or subcommittee.

The complicated history of the legislative veto offers several lessons. It originated and developed for decades by the elected branches without any judicial involvement. When courts became entangled, they could resolve only part of the dispute. If the elected branches valued the advantages of the process before the Court's decision in 1983, they would protect those benefits after the decision. Presidential condemnation of the legislative veto after *Chadha* underscores that the executive branch consists of two separate worlds. One is the macro part (including the White House and the Justice Department) that may find it useful to denounce legislative vetoes as unconstitutional and nonbinding. The other part of government consists of agencies trying to get through the fiscal year as best they can, seeking committee and subcommittee approval whenever they have to.

If presidents, White House aides, and Justice Department officials wanted to push their doctrine of a unitary executive, which places all agencies directly under the president and subject to his orders, executive officials could draft a memorandum and have the president sign it. It would be sent to all agencies, directing them to remove from their budget manuals any language about committee approval. The consequences could be several. Agencies could delete the language but continue to seek committee and subcommittee approval on an informal basis. The result would be some kind of sophisticated game, with the executive branch pretending to honor one model while following another.

There is another possibility. Congress could tell the agencies that if they want spending discretion in the middle of a fiscal year and refuse to seek committee approval, they may adopt the constitutional principles of *Chadha*: comply with bicameralism and presentment. In other words, send your requests to Congress in bill form, get both chambers to pass them, and if the two houses differ in their versions, iron out the differences in conference committee. Then submit the bill to the president for his signature. The frightening uncertainties and burdens of that process have convinced the macro part of the executive branch to limit itself to occasional rhetorical flourishes and leave the agencies alone.

An Open-Ended Process

In a democratic republic, constitutional disputes are necessarily shared between elected and nonelected officials. Yet professors have fallen into the habit of teaching students that the meaning of the Constitution is left to the Supreme Court, which supposedly has unrivaled expertise and authority. For the past half-century the judiciary has promoted that model as well. Government has not functioned that way and should not function that way. It may go in that direction, however, if presidents and members of Congress routinely salute whatever the Court decides. It is remarkable how often presidents and lawmakers criticize a decision, announce that it was wrongly reasoned, and nevertheless accept the result as final. This type of subservient attitude is not healthy for democracy or the courts.

William Howard Taft served in many positions of public office: assistant prosecuting attorney, Ohio superior judge, U.S. solicitor general, federal appellate judge, civil governor of the Philippines, secretary of war, president of the United States, and chief justice of the Supreme Court. In all those positions he saw constitutional law develop at various levels and came to appreciate the virtues and limits of judicial experts. He discovered that often the untutored general public had a better understanding of constitutional law than officials trained in law and assigned to positions of authority.

During his service as a federal appellate judge, Taft wanted courts exposed to unflinching criticism. The right to publicly criticize judicial rulings is "of vastly more importance to the body politic than the immunity of courts and judges from unjust aspirations and attack." Judges would be more careful in their decisions if they understood that each ruling would be subject to candid evaluation, not only by legal practitioners, but by the general public. Taft concluded that if the law "is but the essence of common sense, the protest of many average men may evidence a defect in a judicial conclusion though based on the nicest legal reasoning and profoundest learning."[55]

Writing in 2003, Justice Sandra Day O'Connor observed that if one looks at the history of the Supreme Court and the country over a long period of time, "the relationship appears to be more of a dialogue than a series of commands." Although courts shape the elected branches and the public, the elected branches and the public shape the judiciary. No one should have believed, she said, that the Court's decision in *Roe* v. *Wade* (1973) would have settled the abortion issue "for all time." The ruling triggered violent protests across the country, which O'Connor said was appropriate and expected. She advised that a nation that "docilely and unthinkingly approved every Supreme Court decision as infallible and immutable would, I believe, have severely disappointed our founders." The U.S. Constitution "is not—and could never be—defended only by a group of judges."[56]

For more than two centuries, Congress has played a vital and continuing role in interpreting the Constitution and protecting individual rights. In recent years, however, members of Congress have been too deferential toward court rulings. They need to reassert themselves as a coequal and independent branch of government. Institutional assertion would be healthy for Congress, citizens, and the judiciary.

CHAPTER FOUR
PROTECTING MINORITY RIGHTS

The public understands that Congress legislates on policies for the entire country. There is less appreciation for how it protects the rights of minorities and individuals. To many, it may seem inconceivable that a legislative body voting by majority could ever defend minorities and individuals. How could a majoritarian institution protect isolated and politically weak minorities? The record shows that Congress over the past two centuries has done precisely that. Federal courts, supposedly the "guardians" of individual rights, have not performed as well.

Judicial Guardians?

From James Madison to the present, it has been widely assumed that the judiciary stands as a sturdy sentinel in shielding individuals and minorities from majoritarian abuse. Madison believed that by adding the Bill of Rights to the Constitution, "independent tribunals of justice will consider themselves in a peculiar manner the guardians of those rights."[1] All three branches failed that test by passing and supporting the Sedition Act of 1798. As discussed at the end of the first chapter, the Adams administration and Congress agreed to punish individuals for their criticism of government. Some members of Congress regarded the statute as a blatant violation of the individual right to express personal opinions. Representative Nathanial Macon of North Carolina "could only hope that the Judges would exercise the power placed in them of determining the law an unconstitutional law, if, upon scrutiny, they find it to be so."[2]

Thomas Jefferson wanted federal courts to declare the Sedition Act unconstitutional:"The laws of the land, administered by upright judges, would protect you from any exercise of power unauthorized by the Constitution of the United States."[3] Federalist judges were unlikely to strike down a statute passed by a Federalist Congress and a Federalist administration. The judicial relief desired by Macon and Jefferson never materialized.

For the first century and a half, individual rights were protected almost exclusively by states, Congress, and the president. Nonjudicial institutions were more reliable than the courts. On the rare occasions that issues of individual or minority rights came to a federal court, judges were more likely to side with government and corporations than with individuals seeking justice.[4] In 1937, when the Senate Judiciary Committee rejected a court-packing plan submitted by President Roosevelt, it warned that the proposal "undermines the protection our constitutional system gives to minorities and is subversive of the rights of individuals."

The committee report claimed that the framers "never wavered in their belief that an independent judiciary and a Constitution defining with clarity the rights of the people, were the only safeguards of the citizens." The committee report lapsed into romantic hyperbole:"Minority political groups, no less than religious and racial groups, have never failed, when forced to appeal to the Supreme Court of the United States, to find in its opinions the reassurance and protection of their constitutional rights." The independence of the judiciary was "the only certain shield of individual rights."[5] The record offers scant evidence to support this confidence in the courts.

The performance of federal courts after 1937 has improved, but contemporary studies continue to exaggerate the capacity of courts to protect individual and minority rights. In a famous footnote in 1938, Justice Stone observed that a "more searching judicial inquiry" might be required to protect "discrete and insular minorities."[6] He must have been looking expectantly forward, not backward. For the first century and a half, the process of protecting individual rights was left largely to the regular political process operating outside the courts.

It should not be too surprising that individual liberties would depend on the elected branches. Congress, the president, and state governments have major institutional strengths and responsibilities and are frequently driven by private groups that are well organized and effective in advancing their values, preferences, and agendas. Scholars conclude that the Supreme Court "has not been behaving as the counter-majoritarian force of its textbook description." Instead, it often heeds "quite carefully the policies endorsed by the majoritarian branches of government."[7] Throughout American history, citizens have interacted closely with the elected branches to safeguard individual and minority rights.[8]

In the protection of individual rights, too much attention is directed toward the national government and federal courts. Liberties and rights depend to a great extent on local and state governments. In 1854, the Supreme Court of Indiana held that a "civilized community" could not put a citizen in jeopardy and withhold counsel from the poor. Five years later, the Wisconsin Supreme Court called it a "mockery" to promise a pauper a fair trial and tell him to hire his own counsel. One juror told a judge: "Until the state provided a public defender, he would let everyone go free."[9] The states were far ahead of the national government, including the president and Congress. The U.S. Supreme Court did not recognize those elementary rights until 1963.[10]

During the nineteenth century, jurors provided steady feedback to state legislatures. If jurors considered penalties (especially the sentence of death) too severe for certain crimes, they would simply vote to acquit. State lawmakers were then forced to write new laws to reduce penalties and add sentencing discretion to the criminal process. Otherwise, no matter how much evidence prosecutors could assemble in court, the accused would go free. Citizens checked heavy-handed legislation.

By exercising independent judgment, jurors help redirect government policy, no matter what legislatures enact, prosecutors bring, or courts decide. In the case of obscenity and pornography, the Supreme Court issues very general guidelines about "contemporary community standards." It asks whether something is of "prurient interest," patently offensive, and lacks serious literary, artistic, political, or scientific value. It is up to jurors in various communities to apply those general standards to particular cases involving books, movies, art exhibits, or music performances. The final word is not with legislatures, prosecutors, or judges but with citizens sitting on juries and reaching personal judgments. As explained in the next section, Congress must take into account the values of the community when it legislates.

Conscientious Objectors

The first governmental institution in America to recognize the rights of conscientious objectors was the legislature, not the courts. Lawmakers responded to social needs when they carved out exemptions for those who refused, for religious or ethical reasons, to bear arms. Judges came late to this constitutional issue. In requiring citizens to serve in the militia, colonies and early state governments made exceptions for individuals who expressed religious objections. A Pennsylvania law in 1757 provided that all "Quakers, Mennonites, Moravians, and other conscientiously scrupulous of bearing arms" were entitled, upon the call to arms, to assist in nonviolent ways by extinguishing fires, suppressing the insurrection of slaves and other persons, caring for the wounded, and performing other services. When the Assembly of Pennsylvania passed legislation to create a militia in 1775, it recognized that "many of the good people of this Province are conscientiously scrupulous of bearing of arms," and counseled those willing to join to "bear a tender and brotherly regard toward this class of their fellow-subjects and Countrymen."

On July 18, 1775, the Continental Congress debated proposals to create a militia. It recognized that some people, for religious principles, "cannot bear arms in any case." It asked those individuals to assist "their distressed brethren" by providing assistance "consistently with their religious principles." After the Declaration of Independence, a number of state constitutions, including those of Pennsylvania, Vermont, New Hampshire, and Maine, recognized the rights of conscientious objectors.[11]

During the Civil War, several efforts were made to accommodate individuals who cited religious reasons for refusing to kill. Some Quakers, as a substitute for military service, agreed to serve as chaplains and nurses.[12] Secretary of War Edwin Stanton offered a compromise designed to satisfy both the government and the Quakers. He proposed the creation of a special fund to benefit freed slaves. Any Quaker who paid $300 into that fund would be exempt from military service.[13] That kind of creative proposal could not have come from a court. Congress passed legislation in 1864 to provide that members of religious denominations who, by oath or affirmation, declared they were conscientiously opposed to bearing arms, could be assigned to "duty in the hospitals, or to the care of freedmen."[14]

After the United States entered World War I in April 1917, Congress passed legislation creating a military establishment but stated that nothing in the statute was to be construed to compel any person to serve in the military services who belonged to "any well-recognized religious sect or organization" whose principles forbid its members to participate in war in any form. Implementation of the statute was left to regulations drawn up by the president. An executive order issued by President Woodrow Wilson set forth guidelines on the type of noncombatant service that could be performed by conscientious objectors, including service in the Medical Corps, the Quartermaster Corps, and the engineer service.[15]

When Congress considered similar legislation for World War II, it was understood by that time that individuals could be considered legitimate conscientious objectors who were not members of a religious organization. Initially, House and Senate bills restricted conscientious objectors to members of a "well-recognized religious sect." Two Quakers intervened to insist that the status of conscientious objector depended on individual conscience, not membership in a group. Congress amended the statute to exempt anyone who, "by reason of religious training and belief, is conscientiously opposed to participation in war in any form."[16] That language remains part of current law.

Equal Accommodations

In 1875, Congress passed legislation giving blacks equal access to such public accommodations as inns, land or water transportation, theaters, "and other places of public amusement." Some lawmakers objected that the measure was an effort to make blacks and whites socially equal. Supporters of the bill denied they had that objective. No legislation, they said, could ever direct social relationships. Individuals would associate with the friends they chose. The purpose of the bill was legal, not social. It was designed to give blacks the same legal access to public facilities that whites enjoyed. During House debate, Representative Benjamin Butler of Massachusetts pointed out that the Fourteenth Amendment made blacks citizens of the United States, giving them "a political and legal equality with every other citizen." Nothing in the bill provided for social equality, which continued to "come from the voluntary will of each person." As in the past, each person would select his or her friends and associates. He then moved to the substance of the bill:

> But it is said we put them into the [railroad] cars. The men that are put into the cars and the women that are put into the cars I trust are not my associates. There are many white men and white

women, whom I should prefer not to associate with who have a right to ride in the cars. That is not a question of society at all; it is a question of a common right in public conveyance.

And so in regard to places of amusement, in regard to theaters. I do not understand that a theater is a social gathering. I do not understand that men gather there for society, except the society they choose to make each for himself. So in regard to inns. Inns or taverns are for all classes of people; and every man, high or low, rich and poor, learned or ignorant, clean or dirty, has a right to go into an inn and have such accommodations exactly as he will pay for. . . . I am not obliged to speak to any man or associate with him that I meet at an inn. . . .

The bill is necessary because there is an illogical, unjust, ungentlemanly, and foolish prejudice upon this matter. There is not a white man [in] the South that would not associate with the negro—all that is required by this bill—if that negro were his servant. He would eat with him, suckle from her, play with her or him as children, be together with them in every way, provided they were slaves. . . .[17]

After clearing Congress and becoming law, the bill was challenged in the courts as unconstitutional. In the *Civil Rights Cases* (1883),[18] the Supreme Court struck down the equal accommodation provision. It held that Section 5 of the Fourteenth Amendment empowered Congress to enforce only the prohibitions placed upon the states. It could regulate "state action," but not discriminatory actions by private parties. Dissenting in the case, Justice John Harlan explained that for centuries the common law had prohibited private parties from discriminating against travelers who stopped at inns and restaurants. Railroads were regarded as public, not private, highways. Government authorized them for public use even if private corporations owned and operated them. To Harlan, the rights established by Congress in the 1875 legislation "are legal, not social rights." The right of a black to use the accommodations of a public highway was no more "a social right than his right, under the law, to use the public streets of a city or a town, or a turnpike road, or a public market, or a post office, or his right to sit in a public building."[19] Because of the Court's decision in the

Civil Rights Cases, equal access to public accommodations had to await the Civil Rights Act of 1964.

Women and the Practice of Law

In the years following the Civil War, women entered universities in large numbers to pursue careers in medicine, law, and other professions. Women who possessed a law degree had to seek the approval of a panel of judges (all male) in order to practice law. Routinely they were denied permission. The Illinois Supreme Court refused to grant Myra Bradwell a license to practice law, even though it did not doubt her qualifications. It anticipated that engaging in "the hot strifes of the bar" might tend to destroy "the deference and delicacy with which it is the pride of our ruder sex to treat her."[20] Moreover, the state legislature had not acted to authorize women to practice law. Courts of justice "were not intended to be made the instruments of pushing forward measures of popular reform.[21]

The message was clear. There would be no relief from the courts. Women had to seek rights from legislative bodies. On March 22, 1872, the Illinois legislature passed a bill stating that "no person shall be precluded or debarred from any occupation, profession or employment (except military) on account of sex: Provided that this act shall not be construed to affect the eligibility of any person to an elective office." Also, nothing in the legislation was to be construed "as requiring any female to work on streets or roads, or serve on juries." All laws inconsistent with the 1872 law were "hereby repealed."[22]

Successful at the state level, Bradwell attempted to give women a national right to practice law. Taking her case to the U.S. Supreme Court, she argued that rejection by the judiciary of her application to practice law violated the Privileges and Immunities Clause of the Fourteenth Amendment, which reads: "No State shall make or enforce any law which shall abridge the privileges or immunities of citizens of the United States."

Although the Court in *Bradwell v. State* (1873) agreed that there are privileges and immunities belonging to citizens of the United States, "the right to admission to practice in the courts of a State is not one of them."[23] The right to control and regulate the granting of licenses to practice law in state courts "is one of those powers which are not transferred for its protection to the Federal Government." To that extent, the Court shifted the issue away from the national government and returned it to the states, especially to state legislatures. The right of women to practice law before the U.S. Supreme Court would soon provoke legislation by Congress.

In a concurrence in Bradwell's case, Justice Joseph Bradley expressed some views that were typical of the judiciary (but not for legislative bodies). He argued that the civil law, "as well as nature herself, has always recognized a wide difference in the respective spheres and destinies of man and woman." Man is, "or should be, woman's protector and defender." The "natural and proper timidity and delicacy which belongs to the female sex evidently unfits it for many of the occupations of civil life." He did not point to evidence, unless it was something in nature itself. The family organization, founded in "the divine ordinance, as well as in the nature of things, indicates the domestic sphere as that which properly belongs to the domain and functions of womanhood." This duty to the family "is repugnant to the idea of a woman adopting a distinct and independent career from that of her husband." Bradley observed that it was a maxim of common law that a woman had no legal existence separate from her husband, and that a married woman was incapable, without her husband's consent, of making contracts that would be binding on her or him. He conceded that some women are unmarried but they were exceptions to the general rule. He continued:

> The paramount destiny and mission of woman are to fulfill the noble and benign offices of wife and mother. This is the law of the Creator. And the rule of civil society must be adapted to the general constitution of things, and cannot be based upon exceptional cases.

The humane movements of modern society, which have for their object the multiplication of avenues for woman's advancement, and of occupations adapted to her condition and sex, have my heartiest concurrence. But I am not prepared to say that it is one of her fundamental rights and privileges to be admitted into every office and position, including those which require highly special qualifications and demanding special responsibilities. ... [I]n my opinion, in view of the peculiar characteristics, destiny, and mission of woman, it is within the province of the legislature to ordain what offices, positions, and callings shall be filled and discharged by men, and shall receive the benefit of those energies and responsibilities, and that decision and firmness which are presumed to predominate in the sterner sex.[24]

Whatever one might say about a divine ordinance or the nature of the female sex, Justice Bradley understood that the decision regarding the right of women to practice law would be left in the hands of legislative bodies. Just as the Illinois legislature opened the legal profession to women, so did Congress. In 1878, Congress began consideration of a bill to allow women to practice before the U.S. Supreme Court. Belva Lockwood, who had been admitted to the Washington, D.C., bar in 1873, drafted legislation and worked closely with members of Congress to move the bill through both chambers. The bill provided that when any woman had been admitted to the bar of the highest court of a state, or of the supreme court of the District of Columbia, and was otherwise qualified as set forth in the bill (three years of practice and a person of good moral character, as with male attorneys) she may be admitted to practice before the U.S. Supreme Court. The bill came out of the House Judiciary Committee unanimously and passed the House, 169 to 87, on February 21, 1878.[25]

The Senate Judiciary Committee reported the bill adversely after concluding that it would interfere with the rules of the U.S. Supreme Court, which prohibited women from practicing there. A floor statement on March 18 explained that the committee believed that each federal court had full discretion on the admission of lawyers and that the bill appeared in some cases to favor women over men. Senator Aaron Sargent (R–CA) offered an amendment to delete the text of the bill and replace it with: "That, no person shall be excluded from practicing as an attorney and counselor at law from any court of the United States on account of sex." He pointed out that the District of Columbia and many states had admitted women to the bar. The states included California, Illinois, Michigan, Minnesota, Missouri, North Carolina, Utah, and Wyoming. He thought it was absurd to have female lawyers handle a case in state court and then, if the dispute moved on appeal to a federal court, be forced to transfer the case to a male lawyer.

Sargent recalled that in Shakespeare's time it was impermissible for a woman to appear on stage as an actress. Those parts were performed by men. To have a chance at publication, female writers of great talent had to submit their manuscripts with a male name. He thought it unfortunate for the Court in *Bradwell* to require action by legislatures, "but they seem to have done so, and that makes the necessity for this legislation which I have now offered." The bill was returned to the committee with instructions to report it soon to the floor for debate. Instead, the committee concluded there was no need for the bill and recommended that it be postponed indefinitely. On May 29, Senator Sargent asked that his amendment be reported. He wanted his colleagues to vote, up or down. The initial vote was 26 to 26. Twenty-four Senators were absent. Therefore, the motion to take up the bill was not agreed to.

The bill returned to the Senate floor on February 7, 1879. Once again the Judiciary Committee reported the bill adversely, without written report. Senator Joseph McDonald acknowledged that the Supreme Court might resolve the controversy by a different construction of its rule or by amending it, but "does not seem inclined to do so." Senator Sargent reviewed the progress made by women in entering professions, including medicine and surgery. "No man," he said, "has a right to put a limit to the exertions or the sphere of woman. That is a right which only can be possessed by that sex itself." He then drew a comparison between the rights recently granted to black slaves and the rights still to be recognized for women:

> I say again, men have not the right, in contradiction to the intentions, the wishes, the ambition, of women, to say that their sphere shall be circumscribed, that bounds be set which they cannot pass. The enjoyment of liberty, the pursuit of happiness in her own way, is as much the birthright of woman as of man. In this land man has ceased to dominate over his fellow—let him cease to dominate over his sister; for he has no higher right to do the latter than the former. It is mere oppression to say to the bread-seeking woman, you shall labor only in certain narrow ways for your living, we will hedge you out by law from profitable employments, and monopolize them for ourselves.
>
> Who fears the competition of women? Who pleads for a law to help him hold his medical or legal practice? Let him step down and out. It would be as well to enact that women should not mount the rostrum or pulpit, or engage in writing books in competition with men.[26]

Lawmakers debated what degree of deference should be extended to the Supreme Court to decide its own rules and who should be admitted to practice. Senator George Hoar (R-MA) remarked: "Now, with the greatest respect for that tribunal, I conceive that the law-making and not the law-expounding power in the Government ought to determine the question what class of citizens shall be clothed with the office of the advocate."[27] Suppose, he asked, that the Court decided to prohibit black lawyers from practicing before it, notwithstanding the Civil War amendments. Would there be any doubt that Congress could intercede and pass legislation to reverse the Court? The bill passed the Senate, 39 to 20, and became law. On March 3, 1879, Belva Lockwood was admitted to the Supreme Court bar. A year later she sponsored Samuel R. Lowery, the first southern black to practice before the Court.[28]

The issue of women practicing law was not an isolated and rare example of judicial shortcoming. Not until 1971, in *Reed v. Reed*, did the Supreme Court strike down a law that discriminated against women.[29] The statute invalidated was an Idaho law that preferred men over women in administering estates. In the early decades of the twentieth century, the Court upheld state laws that adopted maximum hours and minimum wages for women, or prohibited women in large cities from working between 10 p.m. and 6 a.m., but this period of "protective legislation" perpetuated the stereotype of delicate women advanced in *Bradwell*.

In *Goesaert v. Cleary* (1948), the Court upheld a Michigan law that prohibited female bartenders unless they were the wife or daughter of the male owner.[30] Writing for the majority, Justice Frankfurter made short work of the legal dispute: "Beguiling as the subject is, it need not detain us for long. To ask whether or not the Equal Protection of the Laws Clause of the Fourteenth Amendment barred Michigan from making the classification the State has made between wives and daughters of owners of liquor places and wives of daughters of nonowners, is one of those rare instances where to state the question is in effect to answer it."[31] In *Hoyt v. Florida* (1961), a unanimous Court agreed that women could be largely exempted from jury service because (echoing *Bradwell*) they are "still regarded as the center of home and family life."[32]

Throughout this period, legal rights for women were advanced by Congress and state legislatures, not the courts. Congress passed the Equal Pay Act in 1963 to prohibit employers in the private sector from discriminating on the basis of sex. Title VII of the Civil Rights Act of 1964 made it illegal for any employer to discriminate against anyone with respect to "compensation, terms, conditions, or privileges of employment" because of the person's sex. Congress passed Title IX of the Education Amendments of 1972 to withdraw federal financial assistance from any educational institution that practices sex discrimination. By the time the Court decided the *Reed* case in 1971, scholarly studies regarded the judicial record as deplorable. According to one study published that year: "Our conclusion, independently reached, but completely shared, is that by and large the performance of American judges in the area of sex discrimination can be succinctly described as ranging from poor to abominable."[33]

Frustration with judicial attitudes reached the point in 1970 when the House of Representatives passed the Equal Rights Amendment by the margin of 350 to 15. After Senate approval, the language submitted to the states for ratification read: "Equality of rights under the law shall not be denied or abridged by the United States or by any State on account of sex." A major advocate of the ERA, Representative Martha Griffiths (D-MI), had this to say during debate in October 1971: "Mr. Chairman, what the equal rights amendment seeks to do, and all that it seeks to do, is to say to the Supreme Court of the United States, 'Wake up! This is the 20th century. Before it is over, judge women as individual human beings.'"[34] A month later the Court decided *Reed*, invalidating a state law that gave preferences to men in administering estates.

Compulsory Flag Salutes

As with other constitutional rights, religious liberty generally depends more on community attitudes and legislative action than it does on court decisions. In *Minersville School District v. Gobitis* (1940), the Supreme Court reviewed a Pennsylvania statute that compelled public school children to salute the American flag.[35] Jehovah's Witnesses adopted a literal interpretation of the biblical injunction against saluting secular symbols: "Thou shalt not make unto thee any graven image, or any likeness of anything that is in heaven above, or that is in the earth beneath, or that is in the water under the earth. Thou shalt not bow down thyself to them, nor serve them" (Exodus 2:4–5). Witnesses regarded the flag salute (extending the right hand, palm upward, toward the flag) as religiously repugnant and saw the gesture as similar to the Nazi salute in Germany. Lower federal courts, drawing attention to the history of religious freedom in Pennsylvania, struck down the compulsory flag salute. The state constitution provided that "[a]ll men have a natural and indefeasible right to worship Almighty God according to the dictates of their own consciences; . . . no human authority can, in any case whatsoever, control or interfere with the rights of conscience."[36]

Yet the Supreme Court in an eight-to-one opinion reversed the lower courts. The decision was issued on June 3, 1940, a time when Nazi Germany was extending its control over Europe. Writing for the majority, Justice Frankfurter appeared to conclude that at such times individual rights must be subordinated to national needs. He argued that individual liberty and national survival required such unifying sentiments as a flag salute. The only dissent came from Justice Harlan Fiske Stone. The top-heavy majority, delivered when the country was on the verge of world war, seemed to be the last word. But several developments made the decision exceedingly fragile.

When the justices returned to the Court after the summer recess, William O. Douglas advised Frankfurter that Hugo Black was having second thoughts about the compulsory flag salute decision. Sarcastically, Frankfurter asked whether Black had been reading the Constitution. "No," Douglas explained, "he has been reading the papers."[37] In addition to Black, Douglas and Frank Murphy had begun to regret joining with Frankfurter. All three had recently come to the Court and looked to Frankfurter for guidance, especially on matters of civil liberties. Within two years they would desert him on this case.

Similar to the Court in *Bradwell,* Frankfurter advised the Jehovah's Witnesses that the relief they sought could come not from the judiciary but from "the forum of public opinion and before legislative assemblies." What Black and the other justices learned over the summer was that newspapers, law reviews, the press, and religious organizations strongly condemned the Court. They accused the Court of violating constitutional rights and buckling to popular hysteria. Frankfurter and his seven colleagues seemed to be adopting oppressive policies from the

Nazis. Of 39 law reviews that analyzed the decision, 31 did so critically. Editorials in 171 newspapers ripped Frankfurter's decision and his reasoning.[38]

This national dialogue had an impact on Black, Douglas, and Murphy. In *Jones v. Opelika* (1942), they recanted from their earlier support for the compulsory flag salute and announced that the 1940 decision had been "wrongly decided."[39] What seemed like an insurmountable eight-to-one majority was now five to four. A change in the Court's composition further undercut Frankfurter's position. Two new justices joined the Court (Wiley Rutledge and Robert H. Jackson) and they joined with Stone, Black, Douglas, and Murphy. Congress also helped undermine the 1940 decision. Legislation passed in 1942 did not support flag salutes. Instead, it provided that "civilians will always show full respect to the flag when the pledge is given by merely standing at attention, men removing the headdress." To the Justice Department, the statute represented a rebuttal of the 1940 decision. The department directed U.S. attorneys to advise local authorities of this new statutory standard.[40]

With *West Virginia State Board of Education v. Barnette* (1943), the Supreme Court had an opportunity to revisit the compulsory flag salute. A six-to-three Court reversed Frankfurter's 1940 ruling.[41] Writing for the majority, Justice Jackson issued a memorable and stirring defense of religious liberty. In striking down the compulsory flag salute, he declared that the "very purpose of a Bill of Rights was to withdraw certain subjects from the vicissitudes of political controversy, to place them beyond the reach of majorities and officials and to establish them as legal principles to be applied by the courts." Powerful sentiments, but much of the credit for changing constitutional doctrine belonged to private citizens, newspapers, law reviews, members of Congress, and attorneys in the Justice Department who recognized that a compulsory flag salute for children was deeply offensive. They did not defer to the Court, even with its imposing eight-to-one majority. In other cases brought in the early 1940s, the Court was more protective of the religious opinions and liberties of minorities, including Jehovah's Witnesses.[42]

The Yarmulke Case

In the 1980s, Congress played a more central role in reversing a restrictive ruling by the Supreme Court on religious liberty. Captain Simcha Goldman of the U.S. Air Force wore his yarmulke indoors on duty for years. An Orthodox Jew and ordained rabbi, he was assigned to a mental health clinic and worked as a clinical psychologist. There was no dispute about wearing a yarmulke until he testified at a court-martial and took a position at odds with the air force. A month later, on May 8, 1981, the air force told him that wearing a yarmulke indoors violated the military dress code.

His first recourse was with the air force, asking it to reconsider its application of the military regulation or rewrite it in a manner that permitted continued use of the yarmulke indoors. The air force declined to provide that relief. He then went to court, asking that a preliminary injunction be issued against the secretary of defense and the secretary of the air force. The district court held that the air force regulation violated his free exercise rights under the First Amendment. The court dismissed the military's claim that allowing Goldman to wear his yarmulke "will crush the spirit of uniformity, which in turn will weaken the will and fighting spirit of the Air Force." A year later, in a separate yarmulke case involving the military, a district court seemed to accept the military's argument that departures from uniformity would adversely affect "the promotion of teamwork, counteract pride and motivation, and undermine discipline and morale, all to the detriment of the substantial compelling governmental interest of maintaining an efficient Air Force."[43]

At the appellate level, all three judges of a D.C. Circuit panel agreed in 1984 that the air force regulation was justified. The military warned that allowing Goldman to wear his yarmulke would trigger religious liberty claims from other military personnel, with soldiers insisting on the right to wear turbans, robes, face and body paint, shorn hair, unshorn hair, badges, rings, amulets, bracelets, jodhpurs, and symbolic daggers. A motion to rehear the case was denied. The case now moved to the Supreme Court.

The rulings by the D.C. Circuit prompted Representative Stephen Solarz (D-NY) to introduce legislation to permit military personnel to wear unobtrusive religious headgear, such as a skullcap, if required for religious reasons. Under his legislation, the secretary of defense could prohibit any religious apparel that interfered with a military duty. The House agreed to the Solarz amendment, even though Representative William Dickinson (R-AL) warned that "we are flying in the face of a court decision just made." Had he looked at the Constitution, Article I expressly empowers Congress to "make rules for the Government and Regulation of the land and naval Forces." The superior judge in this area is Congress, not the judiciary. The Solarz amendment was later removed from the defense authorization bill that became law in 1984.

At the Supreme Court, the brief for the Justice Department defended the air force and argued that support for Captain Goldman would compel the military to choose between "virtual abandonment of its uniform regulations and constitutionally impermissible line drawing." The entire purpose of uniform standards "would be defeated if individuals were allowed exemptions." To disregard the government's interest and permit exceptions "would make a mockery of the military's compelling interest in uniformity." High-flying language, but in fact the military did not insist on total conformity. Without incident, individuals wore a crucifix, Star of David, or other religious symbols on chains placed around their necks.

During oral argument, some justices seemed uncomfortable about telling the Defense Department to rewrite its regulations. Kathryn Oberly of the Justice Department advised them to leave the issue to the elected branches: "If Congress thinks that further accommodation is either required or desirable it can legislate it." If Congress wrote legislation that turned out to be impractical or unwise, it could offer amendments in the future. The Court was not so flexible. Once it recognized a constitutional basis for Goldman's religious liberty it would be awkward in future rulings to redirect court doctrine.

In *Goldman v. Weinberger* (1986), the Court held five to four that the First Amendment did not prohibit the air force regulation.[44] It accepted the military's argument that the outfitting of military personnel in standardized uniforms "encourages the subordination of personal preferences and identities in favor of the overall group mission." Goldman's interests were therefore inferior to the values of uniformity, hierarchy, unity, discipline, and obedience. Justice Brennan, joined by Justice Marshall, wrote a dissent with two conflicting messages. On the one hand he chided the majority for abdicating the judiciary's role "as principal expositor of the Constitution and protector of individual liberties in favor of credulous deference to unsupported assertions of military necessity."[45] He then conceded that the judiciary was not the only institution capable of protecting religious freedom: "Guardianship of this precious liberty is not the exclusive domain of federal courts. It is the responsibility as well of the states and of the other branches of the Federal Government." Having concluded that the Court and the military had refused to grant servicemen their constitutional rights, he identified the remedy: "we must hope that Congress will correct this wrong."[46]

Within two weeks of the Court's decision, legislation was introduced in Congress to permit members of the armed forces to wear items of apparel not part of the official uniform. They could wear any "neat, conservative, and unobtrusive" item that satisfied the tenets of a religious belief. The armed services would retain authority to prohibit the wearing of an item after determining that "it significantly interferes with the performance of the member's military duties." For those who might regard "neat and conservative" as far too vague a standard, those words appeared in existing military regulations.

The House passed the legislation, but the Senate balked. The language was initially tabled, 51 to 49. Senator Barry Goldwater (R-AZ), chairman of the Armed Services Committee, warned that Native Americans would want to wear feather headdresses. He advised soldiers who disliked uniforms to get out of them and join something else.[47] In conference committee, the House provision was eliminated.

Debate continued the next year. Once again the House adopted its amendment. No one spoke against it. Between 1986 and 1987, some of the senators switched their votes. Six senators who had supported the tabling motion (Boschwitz, Burdick, Danforth, Domenici, Harkin, and Rockefeller) now favored the House language. Eight newly elected senators (Adams, Breaux, Daschle, Graham, Karnes, Mikulski, Reid, and Wirth) offered their support. The final vote in the Senate was 55 to 42 for the House amendment.

The comfortable majority in the Senate is remarkable in view of intense opposition around the country. The American Legion, with over 2.5 million members, and the Military Coalition, representing 16 of the largest organizations for military personnel, strongly denounced the House amendment. Secretary of Defense Caspar Weinberger opposed it. A document called a "twenty-star letter" registered intense disagreement. It was signed by five military officers, each wearing four stars: the chairman of the Joint Chiefs of Staff and the other four members representing the army, air force, marine corps, and navy. Congress ignored these grave warnings. The bill protecting the religious liberties of members of the military became law.

Civil Rights Made Real

Those who regard the Supreme Court as the principal guardian of civil rights and civil liberties will think first of the Court's rul-

ing in *Brown v. Board of Education* (1954).[48] A unanimous Court
struck down the "separate but equal" doctrine that emerged in
1896 with *Plessy v. Ferguson*.[49] With only one justice dissenting,
the Court in *Plessy* upheld a Louisiana law that required railroads to provide equal, but separate, accommodations for white
and black passengers. The Court for decades had resisted congressional efforts to secure the rights of black Americans. No
doubt *Brown* marked a major breakthrough in race relations. An
important question: How effective was it in producing social
and political change?

The unanimity of *Brown* cloaked a deeply divided Court. In
1952 and 1953 the justices appeared to be evenly split on what
to do about *Plessy*. Four Justices (Hugo Black, William Douglas,
Harold Burton, and Sherman Minton) were ready to overturn
the 1896 precedent. Five Justices (Fred Vinson, Stanley Reed,
Felix Frankfurter, Robert Jackson, and Tom Clark) did not support overruling *Plessy*. When Chief Justice Vinson died on September 8, 1953, and Earl Warren was confirmed as his successor,
the five-to-four majority now seemed to swing in the direction
of change.[50] For political reasons, reversing a precedent that had
lasted for a half century needed, if possible, a unanimous Court.
What could Warren do to convince four justices to join the
other five?

The strategy was to announce the Court's position not in
one decision but two. In 1954 a unanimous Court declared
racial discrimination in public schools unconstitutional. In stirring language, Chief Justice Warren announced that segregating
children in public schools solely on the basis of race, even if the
physical facilities and other factors were equal, deprived black
children of equal educational opportunities. He concluded that
"in the field of public education the doctrine of 'separate but
equal' has no place. Separate educational facilities are inherently
unequal."[51] Segregation marked a denial of the equal protection
of the laws.

How to implement this new constitutional principle was
pushed to the future. Four justices convinced the majority of five

to give local school districts substantial discretion in putting *Brown* into effect. The Court's ruling a year later, *Brown v. Board of Education* (1955)—referred to as *Brown II*—explained in the opening paragraph: "There remains for consideration the manner in which relief is to be accorded."[52] Full implementation of the principles announced in *Brown I* "may require solution of varied local school problems." School authorities had the primary responsibility for solving the problems and federal courts would have to consider whether their response "constitutes good faith implementation of the governing constitutional principles."[53]

Language in *Brown II* invited substantial delays in putting *Brown I* into effect. A federal judge should consider "a practical flexibility in shaping its remedies and by a facility for adjusting and reconciling public and private needs." Black children should be admitted to public schools "as soon as practicable." The vitality of the constitutional principles put forth in *Brown I*, the Court cautioned, "cannot be allowed to yield simply because of disagreement with them." Yet in directing segregated schools to make "a prompt and reasonable start" in complying with *Brown I*, federal courts "may find that additional time is necessary to carry out the ruling in an effective manner."[54] Courts would have to weigh many factors, including the physical condition of schools, the school transportation system, personnel, and revising school districts and local regulations. The Court directed district courts to implement *Brown I* "with all deliberate speed." Many of the states placed the priority on deliberation, not speed.

Through its language in the implementing decision, the Court encouraged resistance, obstruction, and procrastination. In the decade following *Brown I*, there was little progress in desegregating public schools. As late as 1964, the Court complained that there "has been entirely too much deliberation and not enough speed."[55] In 1964, only 2 percent of black children attended biracial schools in the 11 Southern states. Two years later a federal appellate court remarked: "A national effort, bringing together Congress, the executive and the judiciary may be able to make meaningful the right of Negro children to equal educational opportunities. *The courts acting alone have failed.*"[56] Securing constitutional rights required action by all three branches.

Much of the progress that *Brown I* promised awaited congressional action on the Civil Rights Act of 1964, the most far-reaching statute in this area since the decades following the Civil War. Consistent with public pressures on other constitutional issues, passage of the statute demanded citizens to intervene with years of sit-ins, demonstrations, picketing, and boycotts. The media gave close coverage to harsh police actions against peaceful protesters. The world watched to see if America could reconcile its principles of democracy and equal rights with its practices.

Unlike the limited leverage of a Supreme Court decision, congressional action combined with broad public support could change national policy. Members of Congress held lengthy hearings to explain the need for the legislation. Private citizens testified at those hearings to help inform lawmakers. What emerged from Congress had a legitimacy, solidity, and public understanding that could never come from a judicial ruling. The civil rights bill attracted broad bipartisan support. The House voted 289 to 126 for the legislation; the Senate majority was 73 to 27. Democrats in the House supported the bill 153 to 91. Republican support was even stronger, 136 to 35. The party split in the Senate: 46 to 21 for Democrats and 27 to 6 for Republicans.

Among other features, the Civil Rights Act of 1964 covered public accommodations, the issue that had preoccupied Congress after the Civil War. It prohibited discrimination on grounds of race, color, religion, or national origin if the activity affected interstate commerce or the discrimination was supported by state policy. The activities covered by Congress included restaurants, cafeterias, lunchrooms, lunch counters, soda fountains, gas stations, movies, theaters, concert halls, sports arenas, stadiums, and any inn, hotel, motel, or lodging house open for transient guests. Exempted from the statute were units with five or fewer rooms. Also outside the reach of the statute were private clubs.

The Supreme Court had never overruled the *Civil Rights Cases* of 1883, which invalidated the equal accommodation provision in an 1875 statute. Congress in 1964 offered the Court two justifications: the Fourteenth Amendment and the Commerce Clause. In two unanimous rulings the Court sustained the equal accommodations section.[57] Persistent pressure from the public and Congress eventually prevailed over a nearly century-old judicial ruling. Once again Congress overcame judicial obstacles to protect minorities.

After Congress passed the Civil Rights Act with strong bipartisan support, the Court decided to return to an issue it had earlier ducked. One year after deciding *Brown I*, a mixed marriage case came to the Court. Virginia had passed legislation forbidding miscegenation: marriage or cohabitation between a white person and a member of another race. Given the political climate in 1955 and the uproar in some states to the desegregation decision, the Court decided to sidestep a socially explosive issue. Opponents of *Brown I* predicted that integrated schools would lead to "mongrelization" of the white race. A lower court, in upholding the Virginia statute, said it was necessary for the state to forbid interracial marriages "so that it shall not have a mongrel breed of citizens."[58] Rather than risk further attacks, the Court decided to send the case back to Virginia by citing the "inadequacy of the record."[59] A year later the Court declined to take the case because it was "devoid of a properly presented federal question."[60] In essence the Court decided to buy some time.

The public debate and education that came from congressional action on the Civil Rights Act did much to change attitudes in the country about race. In this new climate, the Court was ready to strike down Virginia's statute and did so in *Loving v. Virginia* (1967).[61] The Court noted that 14 states in the previous 15 years had repealed laws prohibiting interracial marriages. Contemporary public opinion encouraged the Court to accept the case this time and decide it. The Court rejected the argument that Virginia's law should be upheld because the framers of the Fourteenth Amendment did not intend to prohibit miscegenation laws. Under the Constitution, said the Court, "the freedom to marry, or not marry, a person of another race resides with the individual and cannot be infringed by the States." A bold ruling, but the Court would not have issued that decision in 1955. It took political action by Congress, President Johnson, a number of states, and the general public to prepare the groundwork for invalidating racial restrictions on marriage.

In an article in 1962, Chief Justice Earl Warren drew attention to the need for the general public to protect constitutional values and minority rights. Although remembered as an "activist" member of the judiciary, he took care to explain the limits of the courts. In times of emergencies and external threats, the courts may acquiesce to executive and legislative abuses. In particular, he had in mind what happened after World War II with the detention of Japanese Americans, most of them U.S. citizens. Interestingly, he said the fact that the Court held that the actions by President Roosevelt and Congress were constitutional, did "not necessarily answer the question whether, in a broader sense, it actually is." The plain message: The Supreme Court can acquiesce to unconstitutional actions. To Warren, it was a mistake to place too much expectation on the courts: "In our democracy it is still the Legislature and the elected Executive who have the primary responsibility for fashioning and executing policy consistent with the Constitution." The day-to-day job of defending the Constitution also "lies elsewhere. It rests, realistically, on the shoulders of every citizen."[62]

Constitutional law develops not only through the courts but as a result of individuals and groups operating through the executive and legislative branches. Many constitutional disputes are resolved without a lawsuit, although that may be difficult to imagine in our litigious society. Even when an issue is brought before a court there is no assurance it will be decided or resolved there. The judiciary can avoid a constitutional issue, including matters of individual and minority rights, by invoking such threshold tests as standing, ripeness, mootness, and the political question doctrine. If the Supreme Court actually issues a ruling, it must rely on legislative bodies, executive agencies, jurors, and the general public to decide how the new policy will be given effect. At each of these stages Congress plays a central role.

CHAPTER FIVE
CONGRESS AT RISK

To preserve separation of powers and constitutional checks, the framers understood that each branch is responsible for fighting off encroachments and safeguarding its institutional prerogatives. Only through that effort could individual rights and liberties be protected. Maintaining institutional independence is especially crucial for members of Congress. They represent constituents who vote them into office and give meaning to democratic and republican government. For most of its history Congress honored that purpose. In the six decades after World War II, members of Congress began to reveal a lack of confidence, willingness, and interest in defending their institution. Far from being a coequal or even a superior branch, Congress seemed on a downward slide. When Congress does not protect itself, it fails to protect private citizens, democratic values, individual rights, and the system of checks and balances.

The Pendulum Stops Swinging

For most of American history, political power swung back and forth between the executive and legislative branches. Strong presidents were routinely replaced by weak presidents. Congress became ascendant in some periods, weaker in others. This cycle of power changed fundamentally during the Great Depression of the 1930s and World War II. Congress found itself ceding large portions of national policy to the president and executive agencies, shifting the balance not temporarily but permanently. Congress recognized the seriousness of the problem and took steps to reassert itself. Ironically, some of those reforms made Congress weaker.

Massive delegations of legislative power to the executive branch were part of the policies adopted in the 1930s to combat the Great Depression. Congress created new federal agencies and committed billions of dollars to them, offering few details or guidelines. The Emergency Relief Appropriations Act of 1935 appropriated $4,880,000,000 to be used "in the discretion and under the direction of the President." During debate, Senator Arthur Vandenberg (R–MI) expressed his frustration and dismay about the scope of the delegation. The original resolution provided funds for such vague objectives as "relieving economic maladjustment" and "alleviating distress." Vandenberg suggested it would be easier to eliminate even those general purposes and simply enact two sections. The first: "Congress hereby appropriates $4,880,000,000 to the President of the United States to use as he pleases." The second: "Anybody who does not like it is fined $1,000."[1]

A study published in 1937 estimated that Congress, over the previous four years, had given President Roosevelt discretionary authority over the sum of $15,428,498,815. That aggregate compared to a total of $1.6 billion in discretionary spending authority granted to all previous presidents.[2] During his first six years in office, Roosevelt declared 39 emergencies. Representative Bruce Barton (R–NY) remarked: "Any national administration is entitled to one or two emergencies in a term of six years. But an emergency every six weeks means plain bad management."[3]

Congress resorted to secret funding during World War II to develop and produce an atomic bomb. Billions were directed to the "Manhattan Project" to further that objective, with few lawmakers informed of how the money would be spent. Appropriated funds were placed in such general accounts as "Engineer Service, Army" and "Expediting Production."[4] There had been confidential spending in the past, but in small amounts. Congress now took steps in authorizing vast amounts of covert spending and covert operations by the intelligence agencies.

Roosevelt was generally successful in persuading Congress to transfer to him broad legislative and spending authority. If Congress delayed or resisted, he threatened to act without it. He warned lawmakers in 1942 that if they "should fail to act, and act adequately, I shall accept the responsibility, and I will act." In that same announcement he predicted that when "the war is won, the powers under which I act automatically revert to the people—to whom they belong."[5] If the power belonged to the people, and therefore to the people's representatives in Congress, what authority did he possess to act with such independence? Moreover, it was not true that the power reverted to the people after the war. Power remained lodged in the executive branch.

With World War II winding down, Congress began to take stock of itself, especially its constitutional powers over public spending and military commitments. Concern was heightened by the rise of fascism in Europe and Asia and the loss of democratic institutions. At stake, worldwide, was the fate of representative government. Congress understood that it was no longer coequal with the executive branch and had become a second-class, second-rate institution. The Joint Committee on the Organization of Congress, established in 1944, bluntly voiced its concerns:

> Under the Constitution, Congress is the policy-making branch of government. There are manifest growing tendencies in recent times toward the shift of policy-making to the Executive, partly because of the comparative lack of effective instrumentalities and the less adequate facilities of the legislative branch. To redress the balance and recover its rightful position in our governmental structure, Congress, many Members feel, must modernize its machinery, coordinate its various parts, and establish the research facilities that can provide it with the knowledge that is power.

Emerging from the committee's study was the Legislative Reorganization Act of 1946, which restructured congressional committees and offered new analytical tools to lawmakers. The statute directed standing committees of Congress to exercise "continuous watchfulness" over executive agencies. In 1947, Congress terminated 175 statutory grants of emergency and war powers. Some of those provisions dated back to World War I. A number of emergency and war statutes remained in place. In attempting to dial back executive power, Congress inadvertently opened the door to greater presidential power by adopting the United Nations Charter and various mutual security pacts, including NATO. Few people at the time understood that these international and regional compacts would (or could) be used by presidents to initiate war without seeking authority from Congress.

The Impact of the U.N. Charter and NATO

The terrible destruction of World War I brought nations together to form an international body: the League of Nations. Countries joining this organization agreed to submit to it all disputes threatening war and to use military and economic sanctions against nations that practiced aggression. President Woodrow Wilson submitted the plan to the Senate as the Versailles Treaty. A Senate "reservation" to the treaty stated that nothing in the League of Nations could take from Congress its "sole power" under the Constitution to declare or authorize the use of military force against other nations. Wilson's advisers urged him to accept the reservation. He admitted, in a letter to a senator, that no principled objection could be raised against the language. Yet Wilson chose to emotionally confront the Senate, insisting that the reservation "cut the heart" of the treaty and rendered it a nullity.[6] As a result of his stubbornness and rigidity, the United States never joined the League of Nations.

In the middle of World War II, allied nations began to plan for a more effective world organization. Participants in the United States recalled Wilson's failed campaign to join the League of Nations and understood that any commitment of U.S. forces to a world body would require prior authorization by both chambers of Congress. Procedures were drafted to permit the United Nations to use military force against threats to the peace or breaches of the peace. United Nations members would make available to the Security Council, "on its call and in accordance with a special agreement," armed forces and other military assistance. Special agreements would be entered into in accordance with the respective "constitutional processes" of each country.

In a cable from Potsdam, President Truman advised the Senate in 1945 that when any of these agreements were negotiated "it will be my purpose to ask the Congress for appropriate legislation to approve them."[7] There would be no circumvention of the legislative branch. With that assurance, the Senate supported the U.N. Charter by a vote of 89 to 2. To avoid any uncertainty about constitutional principles, Congress passed the U.N. Participation Act of 1945, specifically stating that the agreements "shall be subject to the approval of the Congress by appropriate Act or joint resolution." Statutory language could not be expressed with greater clarity.[8]

Nonetheless, five years later President Truman used military force against North Korea without ever seeking authority from Congress. Never before had a president engaged in a major military commitment without first receiving either a declaration or authorization from Congress. Truman claimed to receive "authority" from two resolutions passed by the Security Council. He told reporters that the military action was not "war" but a U.N. "police action."[9]

This method of circumventing Congress would be used several times. In November 1990, President George H. W. Bush obtained a Security Council resolution to use military force against Iraq, claiming that the resolution made it unnecessary to seek authorization from Congress. Congress passed legislation in January 1991 to support the military action, but Bush in a signing statement argued that he had sought only legislative support, not authority. President Bill Clinton received Security Council support in 1994 to invade Haiti and in 1995 to send U.S. forces into Bosnia. Not once did he seek congressional authority for his military actions.[10]

In the case of the Korean War in 1950, Congress could have defended its prerogatives over war and spending. It chose not to. Instead of fulfilling their oaths to defend the Constitution, lawmakers opted for a different priority: fighting world communism. That choice was not necessary. Members could have resisted aggression in Korea while at the same time protecting the Constitution by telling Truman he needed to come to Congress for authority. Failing to do that, they widened the door for unilateral presidential action and diminished their own institution. This was not the first time that an outside threat was used to place the Constitution in a subordinate position. That pattern began with the Alien and Sedition Act of 1798 and often resurfaces. Violating the Constitution comes with a political price. Just as the 1798 legislation did much to discredit the Federalist Party, U.S. soldiers in Korea became mired in a costly conflict that showed no hope of military victory. The public turned against Truman and elected the Republican candidate, Dwight D. Eisenhower. Having controlled the White House for the last two decades, the Democrats lost the presidential election in large part because of the Korean War.

Another step toward independent, unchecked presidential power came with the adoption of mutual security treaties after World War II. The Rio Treaty of 1947, signed by the United States and 18 countries in Central America, South America, and the Caribbean, promised joint action in the event of military threats. An armed attack against one state was considered an attack against all. The NATO treaty, signed in 1949, represented a pact between the United States, Canada, and 10 European countries. It provided that an armed attack "against one or more of them in Europe or North America shall be considered an attack against them all." In the event of an attack, NATO countries could exercise the right of self-defense. Consistent with the U.N. Charter, the treaty was to be carried out by the parties in accordance with "their respective constitutional processes."

Nothing in the legislative history of NATO anticipated that the mutual security pact would become a substitute for congressional authority, especially for offensive wars. The treaty was explicitly designed for defensive purposes. Under the terms of the treaty, any use of military force would be carried out in accordance with the constitutional processes of the United States, requiring congressional approval by declaration or authorization for offensive actions and any military operations beyond an initial effort to repel sudden attacks.[11] Yet, similar to the misuse of the U.N. Charter, NATO offered another unilateral war-power tool for the president. In 1999, when President Clinton was unable to get the Security Council to support military action against Kosovo, and when Congress refused to provide authority, Clinton circumvented both institutions and used NATO. Instead of seeking approval from elected members of Congress, he sought approval from each of the NATO countries: Belgium, Germany, Italy, etc. The military operation in Kosovo had nothing to do with self-defense.

Congressional "Reassertion"

Truman's military initiative in Korea provoked Congress to reconsider its constitutional role. A report by the House Foreign Affairs Committee in 1951 underscored the profound impact of the Korean War: "The action of the United States in Korea is in one sense unprecedented. For the first time the United States has committed large military forces in a foreign country in response to the action of an international organization. United States forces were committed in Korea by Presidential action."[12] Five years later another House study expressed concern about the growth of presidential war power. Looking back over the past two decades, the study concluded that in no other period "have so many different presidents been called on to exercise this constitutional power [of commander in chief] in so many different kinds of situations, each one of major importance."[13]

President Eisenhower thought that Truman had made a mistake, politically and constitutionally, by going to war against North Korea without seeking authority from Congress. Eisenhower reasoned that joint action by the president and Congress would send the strongest possible message to both allies and enemies. America would be making a military commitment with the support of the legislative and executive branches, not by unilateral presidential action. On New Year's Day in 1957, he met with congressional leaders of both parties to discuss what to do about tensions in the Middle East. House Majority Leader John McCormack (D-MA) asked Eisenhower whether he, as commander in chief, already possessed sufficient authority over military troops without coming to Congress. Eisenhower reminded the lawmakers "that the Constitution assumes that our two branches of government should get along together."[14]

In August 1964, President Lyndon Johnson came to Congress to request the Gulf of Tonkin Resolution to use military force against North Vietnam. He reported that North Vietnam had made unprovoked attacks on American ships, not once but twice. Coming as it did in the middle of a presidential election, no member of the House voted against the resolution. Only two Senators dared oppose it. As with Korea, the overriding value was to unite both branches and both political parties against an outside threat. By demonstrating "resolve" and a common front to an enemy, Congress abandoned any independent role for itself, even to take the time to investigate whether the second attack in the Tonkin Gulf actually occurred (which we now know it did not).

Lawmakers of both parties assumed that passage of the resolution would send an effective warning to North Vietnam, eliminating the need for further military action. A firm stance against aggression, they thought, would prevent a large-scale war. Yet early the next year, after his reelection, President Johnson began to escalate the war in Southeast Asia, eventually placing over 500,000 American soldiers in that region. A huge increase in combat deaths and casualties, joined by massive financial costs and reports of executive branch stealth and deception, turned the country against the war, Johnson, and the Democrats. Like Eisenhower in 1952, Richard Nixon was elected president in 1968 to end an unpopular war. Misguided presidential wars had twice driven Democrats from the White House.

Senator J. William Fulbright (D-AR), who managed the Tonkin Gulf Resolution in the Senate, had written in 1961 that "for the existing requirements of American foreign policy we have hobbled the president by too niggardly a grant of power."[15] Watching with dismay at the widening Vietnam War, by 1967 he could see "great merit in the checks and balances of our 18th-century Constitution."[16] The panel he chaired, the Senate Foreign Relations Committee, released a thoughtful report on the alarming decline of Congress as a separate branch of government. The committee said that if blame is to be apportioned for the expansion of presidential war power "a fair share belongs to the Congress" because of its acquiescence and passivity.[17] The report noted that the United States was unfamiliar with its new role as a world power after 1900. Legislative action was often taken in an atmosphere of urgency, both real and contrived. Members of Congress might have been "overawed by the cult of executive expertise." However, any lawmaker paying attention should have recognized that this pretense of expertise was regularly undermined by a record of executive uncertainty, incompetence, and deception.

Oddly, the committee report claimed that the Senate's rejection of the Covenant of the League of Nations might have created in Congress "a kind of penance for its prewar isolationism, and that penance has sometimes taken the form of overly hasty acquiescence in proposals for the acceptance of one form or another of international responsibility."[18] That analysis was flawed. The failure to join the League of Nations had more to do with President Wilson's stubborn and groundless refusal to accept the Senate reservations. Also, if any branch should be inclined toward "penance" and confess to past errors, it would be the executive branch for entering into wars in Korea and Vietnam without first calculating the costs and the likelihood of failure.

The Senate report stood on firmer ground when it criticized lawmakers for "making a *personal* judgment as to how President Johnson would implement the [Tonkin Gulf] resolution when it had a responsibility to make an *institutional* judgment, first, as to what *any* president would do with so great an acknowledgment of power, and, second, as to whether, under the Constitution, Congress had a right to grant or concede the authority in question."[19] In short, lawmakers forgot what was elementary to the framers: Do not trust people with power. Especially do not trust presidents with the war power, even when they belong to your party. Republicans under George W. Bush would make the same mistake.

Congressional studies led to the drafting of a War Powers Resolution of 1973, intended to give a statutory structure to the commitment of U.S. forces abroad. The House was reluctant to place any advance restrictions on the president. It was willing to recognize that the president "in certain extraordinary and emergency circumstances has the authority to defend the United States and its citizens without specific prior authorization by the Congress."[20] Under the House bill, the president would be required, "whenever feasible," to consult with Congress before sending American troops into combat. He would report the circumstances that necessitated his initiative and why he had not sought prior legislative authority. The House bill allowed presidential military commitments without seeking advance legislative authority.

The Senate regarded the House bill as too permissive and insufficiently protective of legislative and public interests. It decided to identify the precise conditions that would justify unilateral presidential action: a need (1) to repel an armed attack upon the United States and its territories and possessions, retaliate in the event of such an attack, and forestall the direct and imminent threat of such an attack; (2) to repel an armed attack against U.S. armed forces located outside the United States and its territories and possessions and forestall the direct and imminent threat of such an attack; and (3) to rescue endangered American citizens and nationals in foreign countries or at sea. The first situation (except for the final clause) conforms to the understanding of the delegates at the Philadelphia Convention that the president could "repel sudden attacks." The second and third situations reflect later developments of defensive war and protecting American lives and property. The Senate bill required the president to cease military operations within 30 days unless Congress specifically authorized the action.

The bill that came out of conference committee tilted very much toward presidential power. Senator Tom Eagleton (D-MO), who had helped draft the Senate bill, protested that the compromise version gave the president "carte blanche" authority to use military force for up to ninety days. He called it a surrender, a sellout, and "horribly bastardized to the point of being a menace."[21] Nevertheless, the bill passed each chamber. President Nixon vetoed it, but each house had sufficient votes for an override. Many lawmakers interpreted the override as a great triumph for congressional power. They did not read the bill with care to know what they had given away.

The statute has little to commend it. Much of it is dishonest and ineffective. Section 2(a) claims that the purpose of the resolution is to "fulfill the intent of the framers" and "insure the collective judgment" of both branches when U.S. forces are introduced into hostilities. The statute satisfies neither purpose. The framers would have never recognized the authority of the president to use military force against another country for up to 90 days without prior congressional authority. Also, nothing in the resolution "insures the collective judgment." The initiation of military force under the statute is solely by the president. He need only consult with Congress "in every possible instance" before introducing U.S. troops into combat, followed by regular reports.

It is not even clear when the clock starts. According to the resolution, the clock does not start ticking unless the president reports under a very specific section: Section 4(a)(1). No president has reported under that section except Gerald Ford, but by the time he reported to Congress on the *Mayaguez* incident in 1975, the military operation had ceased. Congress could start the clock by passing a statute, as it did in 1983 with the crisis in Lebanon, but it makes little sense to pass a statute to trigger the clock. It simply underscores the weakness of the War Powers Resolution.

A recent effort to replace the War Powers Resolution appears in a 2008 proposal by a war power commission chaired by former secretaries of state James Baker (Republican) and Warren Christopher (Democrat). The study recommends the creation of a 20-person congressional committee, consisting of party leaders, committee chairmen, and ranking members. Except in emergency situations, the president would consult with this select group. That mechanism is unconstitutional. The framers placed the war power with the whole of Congress, from senior lawmakers to junior members, not with some subgroup limited to a consultative function.

If within thirty days Congress has not authorized the military action, the Baker-Christopher proposal calls for two legislative votes. The first would be a nonbinding resolution of approval. That is, Congress would not be called upon to provide legal authority for going to war, just some kind of nonbinding measure. If Congress failed to pass that, it would be required to vote on a binding joint resolution of disapproval. The resolution would go to the president for his signature. If he vetoed it, as expected, Congress would need a two-thirds majority in each chamber to maintain control. In other words, the president could initiate war and continue it provided he had one-third plus one in a single chamber. This proposal, supposedly designed to balance the interests of the two branches, clearly favors the president.[22]

The Impoundment Fight

For the framers, the power of the purse was a fundamental prerogative of Congress. In Federalist No. 58, James Madison said that this power represents the "most complete and effectual weapon with which any constitution can arm the immediate representatives of the people, for obtaining a redress of every grievance, and for carrying into effect every just and salutary measure." Article I, Section 9, of the Constitution vests that power exclusively in the hands of Congress: "No Money shall be drawn from the Treasury, but in Consequence of Appropriations made by Law." In Federalist No. 48, Madison remarked that "the legislative department alone has access to the pockets of the people."

In the years following World War II, members of Congress recognized that great harm had been done to its power of the purse, especially after appropriating vast sums to President Roosevelt with few details to guide actual use. To the extent that presidents took the initiative in war-making as with Korea, or expanded statutory authority as with Vietnam, congressional control over the power of the purse was further diminished. By the early 1970s, Congress faced another challenge from the executive branch. The Nixon administration claimed that the president had no obligation to spend money that Congress appropriated. According to the administration's reasoning, the president could reduce the funds as he liked and even zero out a program. There was nothing new about this dispute over impounding funds. Presidents over the years had often asserted the right not to spend funds. What was new about the Nixon years was the legal theory. The impoundment power was now described as "inherent" in the presidency and thus beyond legislative or judicial checks. Also, no president in the past had claimed such sweeping powers over every facet of the budget, domestic and military.

No one in Congress questioned the right of the president to spend less if the legislative purpose could be fulfilled with less money. But if the power is wielded to cripple or obliterate a statutory project, the president is no longer carrying out his constitutional duty to "take Care that the Laws be faithfully executed." Through this asserted authority, the president in effect exercises an item-veto authority. He could fully fund some programs, drastically retrench others, and cancel programs in their entirety. The question for Congress and the courts was whether appropriations were merely permissive, to be spent entirely under the discretion of the president, or mandatory. About 80 cases went to court. The administration lost almost all of them, including the one that reached the Supreme Court, *Train v. City of New York* (1975).[23] The Court held that Congress in the Clean Water Act had made a deliberate commitment to spend the full amount.

Nixon's claim of inherent impoundment power struck so deeply at the prerogatives of Congress, to both legislate and appropriate, that both chambers fought back strongly. As part of an omnibus budget reform bill, Congress passed legislation in 1974 to limit the president's power. The Impoundment Control Act requires the president to submit two kinds of special messages to Congress when he decides to withhold funds. If he wants to withhold funds permanently and terminate a program, he must submit a "rescission" message. To rescind funds, both houses must complete action on a bill or a joint resolution within 45 days. The burden is entirely on the president to seek support for that legislation. Congress may prevail by doing nothing.

If the president wants to withhold funds temporarily, he must submit a "deferral" message. Deferrals would remain in effect unless one house passed a resolution of disapproval. That type of legislative veto was invalidated by the Supreme Court in *INS v. Chadha* (1983). The Court reasoned that legislative disapproval could not come from a single chamber. Both houses had to disapprove in a bill or joint resolution that went to the president for his signature or disapproval. Federal courts later decided that the one-house veto could not be severed from the deferral authority. If the first was invalid, as a result of *Chadha,* so was the second. Congress in 1987 quickly converted that judicial ruling into statutory law.

Budget Reforms of 1974

After deciding to restrict impoundment, some lawmakers feared that voters would interpret legislative action to mean that Congress was "pro-spending" and thus fiscally irresponsible. To offset that impression, Congress began to look at its budget process. A joint committee on budget control in 1973 associated the growth of budget deficits to procedural inadequacies within Congress: "The constant continuation of deficits plus their increasing size illustrates the need for Congress to obtain better control over the budget."[24] It blamed Congress for its highly decentralized system of committees and subcommittees, with no committee responsible for aggregate numbers and no committee able to match projected spending to projected revenues. It became fashionable to condemn the legislative process for being fragmented, incoherent, and irresponsible.

Those arguments played on stereotypes. The president was considered "responsible" because he headed a centralized and unified branch. The process in Congress was condemned as "splintered": two separate chambers acting on an array of tax, appropriation, and authorizing bills. Part of that fragmented process (two chambers) was constitutional in nature. The framers adopted two chambers as an important check on legislative excesses. It was also a way of reconciling democratic principles (citizens voting directly for House members) with federalism (the Senate protecting the states). The decentralization of Congress also made it more difficult for a president to capture and control all of its parts.

It is a serious misconception to say that Congress in the early 1970s was institutionally unable to comprehend how its separate actions fit into an aggregate budget picture. During that period, the Joint Committee on Reduction of Federal

Expenditures prepared "scorekeeping reports" and circulated them on a regular basis. Legislators knew how congressional action compared to a presidential proposal. Congress took seriously its duty to live within the aggregate amounts of the president's budget. It stayed within the ballpark of those totals while making major changes on individual programs and national priorities. Legislative spending and annual deficits did not spin wildly out of control because of the way Congress was structured before 1974.

Nevertheless, the politics of the early 1970s put pressure on lawmakers to reject "piecemeal" action on tax, appropriation, and authorization bills. The popular catchphrases called for "coordination," "coherence," "comprehensiveness," and a "unified" budget process. To many lawmakers, congressional procedures seemed inferior to the executive process. The Budget and Accounting Act of 1921 had made the president personally responsible for presenting a budget. The statute created a new Bureau of the Budget (now the Office of Management and Budget). The executive budget came nicely bound, unlike the scattered pieces of the congressional process. By 1974, lawmakers assumed that if the president performed better with a centralized process, so would Congress. Yet it was neither wise nor necessary for Congress, functioning as a separate branch with unique institutional qualities, to emulate the president. What were the likely benefits, other than "looking better"? What were the risks?

With the Budget Act of 1974 Congress took the plunge, for better or for worse. The statute created new budget committees and established the Congressional Budget Office to provide the kind of analytical skills that OMB offered to the president. Congress would now pass "budget resolutions" that contained five aggregates: total budget authority, total outlays, total revenues, the surplus or deficit, and the public debt. Outlays and budget authority would be organized by major "functional categories" (such as national defense, transportation, and agriculture) to permit legislative debate on budget priorities. With this legislation, it appeared that Congress had joined the modern world.

Appearances are always complex and certainly that is true of federal budgeting. Increasing the size of a legislative vehicle—from individual tax, appropriation, and authorizing bills to a budget resolution—was of high risk. Why would passing a comprehensive budget resolution automatically usher in responsible action? Why would it protect congressional (or constituent) interests? Operating under the 1974 law, the appropriations committees encountered new problems. Previously, it was in their institutional and political interest to stay below the president's spending proposals to demonstrate that Congress is the more responsible branch.

Under the new system, if the appropriations committees proposed less than the amount allocated to them by the budget resolution, pressures mounted for amendments to bring the total up to the ceiling. Any gap between the total recommended by the appropriations committees and the total allowed by the budget resolution would be quickly filled with projects offered by lawmakers. The Budget Act of 1974 began to legitimize spending that would not have occurred before.

Constituents found it hard to follow the new process. Previously, it was easy. Beginning in 1921, the president proposed a specified amount. Congressional action could be compared to that target. It was either below, above, or the same. Now there are two competing budgets: the president's budget plus the budget resolution. Although the latter might be higher than the president's budget, lawmakers could vote for the amount in the budget resolution and announce that they had "stayed within the budget" (i.e., the congressional budget). In 1979, the chairman of the House Budget Committee, Bob Giaimo (D–CT), admitted that budget resolutions had sanctioned sizable funding increases for program after program, "almost regardless of its effectiveness."[25]

The Era of Deficits

Another unintended consequence of the 1974 budget act materialized in 1981. President Reagan was able to attract a majority of votes from Republicans and conservative Democrats to gain control of the budget resolution in both the House and the Senate. Through that action he possessed a budget tool that enabled him to enforce his priorities: a major tax cut, a large defense buildup, and some cutbacks in domestic programs. The budget resolution was no longer a congressional instrument of control. It was solidly in the hands of the president. Congress had worried about annual budget deficits in the range of $25 billion in the early 1970s. That number was about to explode.

When Reagan entered office, the total national debt (accumulated from 1789 to January 1981) stood at approximately $1 trillion. Much of that amount reflected deficits created by various wars. The result of Reagan's fiscal experiment in 1981 drove annual deficits to several hundred billion a year. By the end of his first term in office, the national debt had doubled from $1 trillion to $2 trillion. By the time he left office four years later, it had tripled to $3 trillion.[26]

It is highly doubtful that this ballooning of budget deficits could have occurred under the previous budget process. Every step of Reagan's proposal in 1981 would have been scrutinized and modified by the tax, appropriation, and authorizing committees. His aggregate policy would have been chopped to bits and radically transformed through this decentralized system of committees and subcommittees. Gaining control of the budget resolution, however, allowed Reagan to achieve his major budget objectives: deep tax cuts and major increases in military spending. There was never a chance that domestic programs could be reduced in size to prevent the deficit from spinning out of control. The politics of 1981 combined with the budget process of 1974 made Congress subordinate to the president. He set the direction, and lawmakers marched to it.

David Stockman, Reagan's OMB director from 1981 to 1985, appreciated how the new congressional budget process promoted White House goals. His book *The Triumph of Politics* (1986) explained that the constitutional powers of Congress "would have to be, in effect, suspended. Enacting the Reagan administration's economic program meant rubber-stamp approval, nothing less. The world's so-called greatest deliberative body would have to be reduced to the status of a ministerial arm of the White House."[27] For the president's plan to work, Congress had to "forfeit its independence."

Reagan's victory over budgeting led to record deficits. After leaving office, Stockman admitted that "a plan for radical and abrupt change required deep comprehension—and we had none of it."[28] All of the confident executive branch predictions of soaring revenues under Reagan's plan fell far short of expectations. Instead of balanced budgets or surpluses, huge deficits appeared. Instead of Congress relying on budget projections from its own CBO, it regularly accepted the administration's flawed and false premises.

Attempts at Deficit Control

Faced with deficits of stunning size, Congress and the administration created a new budget process called the Gramm-Rudman-Hollings (GRH) Act of 1985. The statute publicly admitted that the supposedly superior budget process of 1974 was helpless in dealing with deficits in the range of $200 billion a year. Gramm-Rudman promised to eliminate deficits by fiscal 1991. Starting with a deficit of $171.9 billion for fiscal 1986, the statute commanded a decrease in that level by $36 billion each year over a five-year period. Presto. Under this formula deficits would disappear. The statute further directed the president's budget and the congressional budget resolution to adhere faithfully to those targets. If in any fiscal year a projected deficit exceeded what was allowed in the statute by more than $10 billion, a "sequestration" process would force across-the-board cuts to stay on course. The Senate did not hold hearings on the bill. In the House, four people testified, but I was the only one to analyze the constitutionality of Gramm-Rudman. I told the House panel that Congress could not vest executive duties (sequestration) in a legislative officer (the Comptroller General).

All of the political judgments expected of presidents and members of Congress were now replaced by an abstract, mechanical process designed to achieve deficit control. Gramm-Rudman merely invited further irresponsibility. Costs could be shifted from one year to the next; items were moved off-budget; both sides could invent improbable revenue estimates. Allen Schick, a noted budget expert, correctly observed that Gramm-Rudman "started out as a process for reducing deficits and has become a means of hiding the deficit and running away from responsibility."[29] Both branches routinely practiced deceit in "adhering" to statutory targets. If the president submitted a budget with entirely unrealistic estimates about spending constraints and revenues, Congress was likely to adopt the same phony numbers. Honest and professional estimates would have made Congress look like the "big spender." If the president offered a disingenuous budget, lawmakers eagerly embraced it.

Gramm-Rudman never fulfilled any of its objectives. When it became obvious that deficit targets would not be met by the end of the five-year period, the two branches kicked the can down the road. A new statute, Gramm-Rudman II of 1987, pushed the fantasy forward by two years. By that time, the Supreme Court in *Bowsher v. Synar* (1986) had struck down the procedure used for spending cuts (sequestration).[30] Under Gramm-Rudman II, the deficit for fiscal 1993 was supposed to be zero. It turned out to be $255 billion.[31]

In 1990, former CBO director Rudolph Penner made an interesting observation. He was struck by the fact that in looking at the history of the congressional budget process in the late nineteenth and early twentieth centuries, it appeared to be "chaotic" and yet yielded "balanced budgets or surpluses most of

the time, unless there was really a good reason to run a deficit."
The budget process in place after 1974 "looks very elegant on
paper, but it is leading to very dishonest and disorderly results."[32]

Item Vetoes and Balanced Budgets

Some members of Congress began to regard the rescission procedure of 1974 as too restrictive on the president. As a means of
gaining better control over the budget deficits of the Reagan
years, they wanted to authorize some type of item-veto authority for the president. Strangely, presidential irresponsibility was
to be rewarded with new budget powers. Different proposals
emerged. One approach was called "expedited rescission." It
required Congress to vote on a president's proposal to rescind
funds. Lawmakers could no longer sit on their hands when the
president recommended rescissions (as the 1974 statute permitted). Under expedited rescission, if one house took a vote and
disapproved, obviously that would be the end of it. There would
be no purpose for the other house to act. Approval of both
houses would be necessary. The House of Representatives
passed bills for expedited rescission in 1992, 1993, and 1994. The
Senate did not act on those proposals.

In 1995, Republicans gained control of the House of Representatives and began to push an alternative more favorable to
presidential power. It was called "enhanced rescission." Instead of
the burden being on the president to get both houses to support
a rescission proposal, the burden would be reversed. Presidential
proposals would become law unless Congress passed a resolution
of disapproval within a fixed number of days. If Congress failed
to act during that period, the rescissions would take effect. If
Congress passed a resolution of disapproval, it would go to the
president and face a likely veto. If vetoed, it would take two-
thirds of the members of each house to restore the funds.

The House passed the enhanced rescission bill in 1995. The
Senate agreed to pass a different measure and the two chambers

settled, the next year, on a modified form of enhanced rescission. Before a Senate committee, I testified that Congress should not surrender its power of the purse to the president. Under the new law, the Line Item Veto Act of 1996, the burden was on Congress to disapprove presidential rescission requests during a 30-day period. In addition to rescissions of discretionary appropriations, the president could also cancel any new item of direct spending (entitlements) and certain limited tax benefits.

The shift of constitutional authority seemed quite extraordinary. However, in terms of presidential cuts and deficit control, the statute had minimal effects. The total savings achieved by President Bill Clinton, over a five-year period, came to less than $600 million. His cancellations for fiscal year 1998 represented about $355 million out of a total budget of $1.7 trillion. Although the budgetary reductions were minor, the damage done to Congress as a coequal branch was substantial. The statute basically announced: "Lawmakers are irresponsible and unable to control their appetite for spending. We need the leadership and fiscal responsibility of the president to protect the national interest." In 1998, in *Clinton v. City of New York*, the Supreme Court struck down the Line Item Veto Act as a violation of the legislative procedures set forth in the Constitution.[33]

Anyone familiar with budgetary policy over the last two centuries would be surprised at lawmakers championing the president as a fiscal guardian. The driving force behind large increases in federal spending has generally been the president, certainly from the 1930s to the present. To a great extent that is because of presidential wars in Korea, Vietnam, and Iraq. But presidents have also been behind such initiatives as Eisenhower's federal highway program, Kennedy's plan to send a man to the moon, Johnson's "Great Society" programs, and Reagan's defense buildup.

Over his eight years in office, George W. Bush allowed federal spending to rise dramatically, fueled in part by the Iraq war but also reflecting generous increases in domestic and international programs. Mickey Edwards, former House Republican from Oklahoma, wrote a book in 2008 entitled *Reclaiming Conservatism.* He expressed dismay at the lack of fiscal discipline during the Bush years. The federal deficit, he pointed out, "mushroomed, and not only because of the wars in Afghanistan and Iraq."[34] Republicans have attributed their defeats in the 2006 and 2008 elections in large part to their failure to exercise fiscal discipline. Democrats may suffer the same kind of losses in the 2010 and 2012 elections if they acquiesce to heavy spending and large deficits by the Obama administration.

Some Reform Proposals

Congress has successfully blocked action on some proposals that would have weakened budgetary control. Throughout the 1980s and 1990s, members of Congress debated a constitutional amendment to require a "balanced budget." In 1984, President Reagan claimed that a balanced budget amendment "would force the Federal Government to do what so many States and municipalities and all average Americans are forced to do—to live within its means and stop mortgaging our children's future."[35] His claim of fiscal responsibility by states and municipalities was extremely misleading.

There are several drawbacks to a balanced budget amendment. As with line-item proposals, congressional efforts to pass an amendment and send it to the states for ratification would send a clear message to the public that lawmakers are unable, or unwilling, to control federal spending. In 1995, Representative Gerald Solomon (R-NY) told the House: "Madame Speaker, Congress has repeatedly shown that it is not prepared to deal responsibly with the problems without some kind of a prod. The enactment of a balanced budget amendment will help to give Congress—and this is the point—it will help to give Congress that prod, that spine, that backbone and, for some who need it, the excuse to do what the American people have to do, and that is to live within means."[36]

However appealing a constitutional amendment might seem, it is easy to predict that a balanced budget requirement would not produce a balanced budget. In testifying before a House committee in 1992 and a Senate committee in 1994, I urged lawmakers to look at the states and their history of balancing budgets. What states have done over the years is to spawn two budgets: an operating budget (balanced) and a capital budget (authorizing indebtedness). If states actually balanced their budgets by limiting expenditures to available or projected revenues, we would not hear of state and municipal bond offerings or states worrying about their bond ratings. Much of the borrowing by state and local governments goes for capital expenditures for roads, education, sewerage, housing, and urban renewal.

Congress would have little trouble coming up with an "operating budget" that is in balance while transferring many expenditures to a "capital" budget. States have the advantage in relying on the federal government for much of their budgetary needs, ranging from federal grants each year (about one-fifth of state revenues) to extra federal assistance in time of natural disasters. In 2009, states gratefully received billions in federal funds as part of the economic stimulus package. Were Congress to adopt a "balanced budget," its power and prestige would suffer when citizens discovered that lawmakers (assisted by executive officials) had performed a cynical accounting trick.

After the Supreme Court invalidated the Line Item Veto Act, Congress debated substitute proposals. One idea, explored at a House subcommittee hearing in 2000, was to amend the Constitution. Under consideration was language adopted from a state constitution to authorize the president to item veto "any appropriation or provision." I pointed out that at the state level that kind of language is effective because appropriations are made for discrete amounts. It is not unusual to see state bills with amounts as small as $2,000. But the federal government does not appropriate with that detail. Appropriations accounts typically provide lump-sums in the billions. If the language above were added to the U.S. Constitution, presidents would not find any appropriation "items" in the bills submitted to them.

The proposal submitted to the House subcommittee in 2000 did not define "provision." Would it apply to conditions placed on appropriations and other nondollar language? In exercising this type of item veto, could a president convert a conditional appropriation into an unconditional appropriation and eliminate the restriction that Congress had all along intended? Borrowing language from state constitutions is often misleading. Part of the reason for giving governors an item veto was that most legislatures were part-time institutions. They met every other year and when they did assemble it was for a few months. Those conditions forced state legislatures to delegate to the governor substantial discretion, including the power of an item veto. Congress has met in annual session ever since 1789 and its sessions in the modern era are almost year-round.

In 2006, the House and Senate Budget Committees held hearings to consider an item-veto bill designed to satisfy the Supreme Court's ruling in *Clinton v. City of New York*. The legislation would authorize the president to propose the rescission of any dollar amount of discretionary budget authority or rescind, "in whole or in part," any item of direct spending (entitlements). Once those proposals were submitted to Congress, an expedited process would require lawmakers to vote up or down within a fixed period of time. No amendments by lawmakers would be permitted, either in committee or on the floor. The essence of legislative authority is the capacity to shape a product. Under this item-veto proposal, the president could do that. Congress could not. Also, the rescission legislation would give presidents substantial control in driving and dictating the congressional schedule.

In testifying at these hearings, I concluded that the procedure mapped out above would probably satisfy *Clinton*, but lawmakers have a duty that goes beyond drafting bills acceptable to the Supreme Court. They need to ask: Does the legislation protect the powers and reputation of Congress as a coequal branch?

The answer does not come solely from court rulings. It lies in the willingness of each lawmaker to determine what Congress must do to preserve its place in a system of coordinate branches. The true expert here is the lawmaker, not the judge. No one outside the legislative branch has the requisite understanding of congressional needs or can be entrusted to safeguard legislative or national interests.

A lawmaker need not be an attorney to decide such questions. Someone without a law degree is just as able and experienced in judging what Congress must do to protect representative democracy and the rights of citizens and constituents. Just as Congress should not consciously pass an unconstitutional bill, so should it not pass legislation that damages itself. The item-veto legislation considered in 2006 would have damaged the institutional interests of Congress in several ways.

First, it sent a clear message to the public that Congress has been irresponsible with its legislative work, both in the level of spending and the particular provisions it placed in bills. To correct those supposed defects, Congress would sanction a fast-track procedure that enables a president to publicly identify wasteful projects and force congressional votes. By selecting that process lawmakers advertise their incompetence to perform constitutional duties. That is Damage No. 1.

On what grounds can it be said that the president has a unique and superior capacity to look at bills presented to him and judge which items lack merit? Would those judgments be actually made by the president or by aides and even private individuals and groups who want to reverse a congressional decision? Are they more qualified than lawmakers to determine what should be allocated to particular districts and states? No. Would their judgments be based on nonpartisan, rational analysis or strongly tilted by political and partisan objectives? Generally the latter. It is unclear how a president would credibly put together a list of proposed rescissions.

Whatever the merits or demerits of the president's selections, he would probably receive public credit for "fighting against waste." Few voters and constituents would have the time or expertise to examine each item on the president's list. It is difficult to distinguish between "justified" and "unjustified" programs. The president may win on image alone, not on substance or convincing analysis. At the same time, Congress would receive a public rebuke for having enacted the supposedly wasteful items (Damage No. 2).

What of the next stage? If Congress were to disapprove the rescission proposals, it would be criticized for not supporting the good-faith efforts of the president. It would be an easy matter for the president to condemn Congress for establishing a fast-track procedure to correct for its deficiencies and then refuse to delete unwanted and unneeded funds (Damage No. 3). If Congress has an interest in building public support and credibility, this is a process to avoid.

Finally, consider the politics of this form of line-item veto authority. The president would have a new tool to coerce lawmakers and limit their independence. He or his aides could call members of Congress to alert them that a particular project in their district or state might be on a list of programs scheduled for the rescission list. During the phone conversation, the member would be told that the administration actually thinks the project is a good one and should be preserved. The member is assured that the administration will do everything in its power to see that the project is kept off the list. At that point the conversation shifts ever so slightly to another topic. The member is asked whether he or she is willing to support a bill, treaty, or nomination desired by the president. The lawmaker is at a distinct disadvantage. To preserve the project in a state or district, it may be necessary to support a presidential program that lacks merit. Perhaps both sides sign off to this deal, pushing spending higher (without the public ever knowing). The political leverage of this process diminishes the constitutional independence of Congress (Damage No. 4).

Of course one final action would further degrade Congress as an institution: voting in favor of the president's rescission list.

The president would receive full credit for guarding the purse. Congress gets a pounding for having ever included the items. It's possible that the projects were more than justified, but lawmakers chose to capitulate to an angry public. These events would be costly sideshows, highly damaging to Congress and bringing insignificant relief to budgetary problems.

To control budgets and deficits, Congress has more effective ways than enacting line-item veto authority or passing balanced budget amendments. Much more profound would be a refusal to authorize military commitments unless the need is clearly urgent, supported by reliable information, and subject to independent investigation by Congress and outside parties. The Vietnam War and the current Iraq War caused profound damage to the national budget. Congress should have insisted that UN inspectors be sent to Iraq before it acted on authorizing legislation. Strategic errors of that magnitude require generations for recovery.

Presidents have sufficient constitutional powers over the budget. Through the regular veto power, presidents can tell Congress that unless it strips certain items from a bill that is in conference committee, they will exercise the veto. Threats of that nature are regularly employed to shape the contents of legislation. The president may announce that if a bill exceeds a particular total he will veto it, again putting pressures on lawmakers to modify the bill to meet the president's satisfaction.

More important than the veto power is the budget the president submits. Under the 1921 statute, he is supposed to submit a "responsible" budget. It is within the president's power to recommend a bill that balances expenditures and revenues. The historical record provides strong evidence that the aggregate numbers submitted by presidents (total spending, deficits and surpluses, etc.) are generally followed by Congress, and that legislative changes have more to do with priorities than totals. The key to fiscal discipline is a president who submits a responsible budget. Without that leadership, all other reform proposals are superficial diversions.

Congress effectively challenged the Nixon impoundments and has, fortunately, decided against a balanced budget amendment and recent item-veto proposals. The experience with the Gramm-Rudman bills was a healthy reminder that statutory mechanisms, no matter how ingenious, are no substitute for the individual and collective judgments required of elected officials.

CHAPTER SIX
SAFEGUARDING DEMOCRACY

From World War II to the present, Congress has lost much of its independent capacity to legislate, monitor executive agencies, and protect its powers. Parliamentary bodies around the globe have experienced similar declines. The damage is not merely to one branch of government but to the entire democratic system. When Congress is weak, so are constituents and so is their trust in government. If members of Congress want to restore their institution to coequal status and gain the respect of other branches and constituents, constructive steps are available.

A Separate Branch

Little can be accomplished unless a basic shift occurs in legislative attitudes. Members of Congress and their staffs must view themselves as part of a separate branch with distinct and nondelegable duties, procedures, and customs. Without that basic understanding there can be no system of checks and balances. The structural safeguards intended to protect individual rights and liberties disappear. Lee Hamilton, drawing on thirty-four years of public service in the House of Representatives as a Democrat from Indiana, observed: "It is one of the American system's marks of genius that we always have one branch keeping an eye on the other."[1] Much of Congress's decline over the last six decades is rooted in lawmakers identifying themselves not with their own branch but in deferring to the president and the judiciary. Being coequal requires independent judgment, not acquiescence and submission. As noted by political scientists Thomas Mann and Norman Ornstein, contemporary lawmakers "simply do not identify strongly as members of the first branch of government."[2]

Independent Spirit

When members of Congress take the oath of office to defend the Constitution, it is as they see the Constitution, drawing on their personal analysis and the understandings they bring to public office. They come to Congress as former governors, mayors, state lawmakers, physicians, farmers, engineers, and other professions. Their view of government and public affairs is unmatched by the other branches. It is appropriate for lawmakers to be guided and informed by the Supreme Court and the president, but not to the point of losing capacity for independent judgment and action. Otherwise, we would still be stuck with the Court's reasoning in *Dred Scott* and its cramped constitutional rulings on child labor, the right of women to practice law, the legislative veto, religious liberty in the military, and other issues. Without institutional autonomy, lawmakers would bow to overblown claims by presidents and federal courts about their "plenary" powers. No doubt there are personal risks for lawmakers who publicly object to presidential and judicial positions, but the risk is far greater when Congress capitulates and falls silent.

Institutional Pride

A spirit of independent inquiry must originate with lawmakers. They need to communicate that value to aides who serve in personal offices and committees. Some years ago I listened to a talk on congressional oversight by David Skaggs, former Democratic House member from Colorado. He asked the audience: "How many of you work in a member's office?" A number of hands shot up. Next: "How many work on committees?" A show of more hands. Third question: "How many of you are proud to work for Congress?" After a pause, a few uncomfortable hands appeared. I became a congressional staffer in September 1970. If anyone had asked the third question to a room of staffers then, the response would have been quick and positive. We understood that whatever the faults of Congress, we supported the legislative branch and the system of checks and balances.

Outside Help Needed

Strengthening Congress will require the combined efforts of scholars, private organizations, the media, and other participants. Justice Brandeis in 1927 reminded us that the "greatest menace to freedom is an inert people."[3] Self-government requires continued participation by the public. It is easy for citizens to poke fun at Congress; most of its actions are in public view. If the process of reaching decisions in the other branches were more visible, we would have a far less favorable opinion of presidents, executive officials, and federal judges.

Citizens need to do more than turn out for elections. Working individually and with others, they can press for change and are often successful.[4] Private organizations, through litigation, congressional testimony, and independent investigations, can provide a type of checks and balances that one would expect to come from collisions among the three branches. If political institutions fail to do that job, because of passivity or deference, the burden on private citizens and groups is all the greater.

The goal is to restore not merely Congress as an institution but democratic values and the principle of self-government. Moving away from the current concentration of power in the presidency and the Supreme Court is a necessary structural step to protect individual rights and liberties. At town hall meetings, constituents can ask lawmakers if they are fulfilling their oath to the Constitution by exercising independent judgment or simply taking direction from other branches. In their recent book, Frederick Schwarz and Aziz Huq correctly advise: "Voters, both Democratic and Republican, must ask their candidates whether they are willing to fulfill their constitutional responsibilities."[5]

Congressional action is easier when assisted and spurred by a national consensus. Individuals throughout the country are part of the process that debates issues and demands change. At times Congress and the president get credit for enacting a federal program when the origin was rooted in pressure that began in local communities, spread to the states, and exerted such national force that elected officials responded with public laws and effective oversight.

What the Party Asks

The willingness of individual members of Congress to think and act independently depends on how their institution is structured and organized. If the Speaker of the House gains effective control over the legislative agenda, lawmakers may be asked to suspend individual views to support "party unity" or the "interests of the president." Congress is weakened as an institution when party unity becomes the dominant value, both in supporting a president's program or in opposing it. Individual doubts and judgments are put to the side. Majority leaders in Congress may insist that the president's program "trump everything."[6] The all-inclusive "everything" can include the Constitution. At that point the legislative branch loses its separate character and functions as an arm of the executive branch, unable or unwilling to exercise checks and balances.

If the president's agenda is seriously misguided (e.g., Lyndon Johnson's war in Vietnam and George W. Bush's intervention in Iraq), the price is heavy. Not only do the president and the nation suffer but so does the president's party in Congress and so do the reelection chances of the members of that party. Roy Blunt (R-MO), who served as House Republican Whip from 2006 to 2008, later reflected: "I think you can argue that our leadership was too close to President Bush."[7] Party leaders, preoccupied with strategic interests, can lose touch with their party base and even their own leadership team.[8] A member of Congress takes a solemn oath to the Constitution, not to the president, the Supreme Court, or a political party. The oath is informed and directed by personal values and one's conscience. The oath is inescapably individual, not part of a group exercise.

On one occasion I met with seven House members after their party won the presidency. Because they also controlled Congress, I said they needed to provide close oversight of the executive branch. If they did not, the White House would get in trouble and eventually so would their party and their colleagues in Congress. If the other party controlled both branches, I would have offered the same advice. The seven members and their party colleagues chose to put their trust and loyalty in the president. Several years later, after the president had gotten in trouble and their party suffered at the polls, we met again. They shook their heads at their failure to exercise institutional checks. Heedless loyalty to a president runs against the Constitution, legislative powers, party interests, and the chances for reelection by members of that party. If members of Congress mechanically salute to whatever a president wants, they stop being representatives and become White House aides.

What We Owe the President

Representative Jim Wright recalls how he and Speaker Tip O'Neill helped President Ronald Reagan on matters of foreign affairs: "He was our President. We owed him that."[9] Lawmakers owe the president independent and informed judgment, not deferential loyalty. No president says: "This is my Congress. I owe it that." Members of Congress weaken their institution and democratic government when they decide to "close ranks" on issues of foreign affairs and national security. Another platitude guaranteed to enfeeble Congress: "Politics stops at the water's edge." No. Politics—in the sense of exercising informed judgment—continues. O'Neill initially advised that "when it comes to foreign policy, you support your president."[10] By September 1967 he turned against President Johnson and the Vietnam War.[11]

During the Cuban Missile Crisis of 1962, President Kennedy sought and received congressional support. Speaker Carl Albert agreed with that legislative attitude: "He was our president."[12] No matter what misgivings might have surfaced privately, lawmakers remained loyal. Two years later, Albert began to learn the costs of automatically uniting behind presidential military action. In response to two reported attacks by North Vietnam in the Gulf of Tonkin (the second "attack" never occurred), the House unanimously and the Senate with only two negative votes passed a resolution giving President Johnson broad authority to use military force. The costs were military, constitutional, political, and economic. Funds planned for the War on Poverty went to Vietnam, Republicans picked up 47 House seats in 1966, and the war created bitter divisions among Democrats, helping Richard Nixon win the presidency in 1968.[13]

On December 12, 2000, the Supreme Court in *Bush v. Gore* put an end to recounts in Florida and helped usher George W. Bush into the White House.[14] Few Democrats, Republicans, liberals, or conservatives can view the Court's reasoning as anything other than unprincipled and ad hoc, but the country "united" behind the Court and the new president.[15] In his concession speech the next day, Al Gore announced: "Now the U.S. Supreme Court has spoken. Let there be no doubt, while I strongly disagree with the Court's decision, I accept it. I accept the finality of this outcome."[16] He added: "This is America and we put country before party. We will stand together behind our new president."[17]

Perhaps the effort to place country over party seemed patriotic, but the country, democracy, and the Constitution all suffer by mindlessly saluting a Supreme Court ruling regardless of its merits. It is also pointless to "stand together" behind a new president. Stand lockstep without offering independent judgment or exercising necessary checks and balances? Keep criticism and doubts to oneself? Such conduct converts the president into an imperial force. That kind of attitude was present in October 2002 when Congress passed a resolution authorizing military action against Iraq without any reliable evidence that Iraq possessed weapons of mass destruction or presented any sort of national security threat to the United States.

Campaign Finance

For lawmakers to act independently and exercise checks and balances, fundamental changes in campaign financing are required. The time needed for effective legislation and oversight is consumed by each member raising money for his or her race or party. Fund-raising becomes a part of every day spent at home and every day in the nation's capital. In a floor statement on January 6, 2009, Senator Robert C. Byrd (D-WV) recalled the dramatic shifts in money needed for election and reelection. In 1958, he and Jennings Randolph (D-WV) spent a combined $50,000 to win their Senate seats in West Virginia. Today, driven by the costs of radio and television ads, Senator Byrd estimated that senators "can expect to spend about $7 million."[18] Members tell me that half of their time, and even more, is spent raising money. In the chase for dollars, some lawmakers step over the line and land in prison. For the great majority who avoid illegal conduct, precious hours needed to fulfill constitutional duties are lost.

Congressional efforts to control campaign expenditures are limited by the Supreme Court's decision in *Buckley v. Valeo* (1976), which concluded that money is "speech" and therefore entitled to constitutional protection.[19] Several justices at the time rejected the Court's analysis, and justices ever since have sharply repudiated the supposed link between money and First Amendment interests. They recommend that national policies over campaign funding be left to the elected branches. Congress has every right to hold extensive hearings to determine whether *Buckley* needs to be overruled, especially in light of more than three decades of experience. Congress has more competence, authority, and legitimacy in this area than the Court. Independent analysis by Congress can justify lawmakers telling the Court: "With all respect, you got it wrong. We are passing new legislation to regulate political campaigns. The level of spending is corrupting our political system and weakening Congress as an independent branch."

Legislative Staff

Congress needs to take a fresh look at the salaries and incentives of congressional staff. Many of the top positions in the offices of representatives and senators and on legislative committees receive adequate pay. Other staff salaries are much too low, especially in a city as expensive as Washington, D.C. Pressures are intense and hours are long.[20] The temptation is great to work a few years, add the congressional job to one's resume, and move on. Congress needs to retain these talented staffers and the skills they have acquired. A half-century ago it was not unusual to see staffers devote their professional careers to a congressional committee. That is less the case today.

Hackneyed Debates

Much of the criticism aimed at Congress is preoccupied with trite complaints. There is nothing wrong with "lobbyists" and "special interests" trying to influence government. From 1789 forward, they have exercised pressure on all three branches. It is their constitutional right to participate and bring information and perspective to the political process. Individuals who strongly condemn lobbyists and special interests will inevitably make exceptions for their own favorite organizations. Broadsides against lobbyists and special interests have little meaning and are not helpful in shaping or debating public policy. The remedy comes not from eliminating this type of public participation but making it visible and avoiding the corruption that can occur.

It is similarly unhelpful to condemn Congress for "pork-barrel" spending or for engaging in "earmarks." Some projects are wasteful and damage the reputation of Congress, as with Alaska's famed "bridge to nowhere." Certain earmarks should be prohibited, such as funneling money to a company that contributes to a lawmaker's campaign or sending public funds to a lawmaker's family.[21] Informed criticism of earmarks would require a detailed analysis of each project in each district and state. That effort would find merit in many projects.

Lawmakers have every right to direct spending to their districts or states. There is no reason in a system of representative government to shift those decisions from elected officials to executive officials. Nor are there any grounds to think that agency employees, in allocating funds, will be more expert or less immune from partisan and political pressures. The remedy, as with lobbying and special interests, is to assure full visibility before projects are authorized and funded.

Earmarks are commonly defined as "congressionally directed spending." The public and the press should pay comparable attention to "presidentially directed spending." Newspaper stories will highlight a congressional earmark of $50,000 to construct a National Mule and Packers Museum in Bishop, California. Take a look at presidential spending and you will see some really huge figures, such as $13 billion for 28 presidential helicopters.[22] Some reformers insist that each congressional earmark be not only funded but specifically authorized. Much of executive spending, such as foreign assistance, does not receive regular authorizations.

Public outrage at lobbyists, special interests, earmarks, and special projects takes the focus off of significant issues and obsesses on minor ones. In 2009, lawmakers rebuked AIG for giving $165 million in retention bonuses to its employees. Additional criticism was leveled at the approximately $7.7 billion covering 8,500 earmarks in the omnibus spending bill enacted in March 2009. Those were legitimate targets for public debate. Yet a story in the *New York Times* that same month described phenomenal sums wasted in the Defense Department for weapons programs. Nearly 70 percent of the programs were over budget for a combined total of $296 billion.[23] That problem persists decade after decade with little improvement. Fewer cases of fraud and corruption involving military contracts are sent to the Justice Department for prosecution. The number of employees in the Defense Department tasked with identifying and correcting fraud and corruption has been cut substantially in recent decades.[24] If constituents want Congress to take action to eliminate waste, that is one area of opportunity. Many others deserve close and continuing scrutiny.

Using Legislative Weapons

Members of Congress have many powerful tools to protect their prerogatives, but they have to use them. In 1986, President Reagan nominated William Rehnquist to move from associate justice of the Supreme Court to chief justice. The Senate Judiciary Committee asked the administration for certain memos that Rehnquist had written when he headed the Office of Legal Counsel in the Justice Department. As expected, the administration told the committee that the memos could not be released because they were part of the internal deliberative process. That marked step one in the confrontation. The committee then played its card, announcing that Rehnquist would not be reported from committee until it received the documents. Not only would there be no floor vote on Rehnquist but no floor vote on Antonin Scalia as associate justice. The Senate planned to take up the two together. The administration understood the committee's leverage and released enough memos to satisfy Senate needs.[25]

During the Reagan years, the two branches collided over the president's power to "reinterpret" a treaty. Could the administration arrive at a meaning of a treaty contrary to what the Senate understood at the time it granted approval? The Reagan administration promoted an expensive antimissile shield consisting of satellites armed with laser weapons. Executive officials referred to it as the Strategic Defense Initiative (SDI). The press called it "Star Wars." Some members of Congress objected that deployment or even testing of SDI would violate the Antiballistic Missile (ABM) treaty with the Soviet Union. The complex debate about treaty interpretation came to an abrupt halt when Congress enacted legislative language prohibiting the secretary of defense from deploying any ABM system "unless such deployment is specifically authorized by law after the date of the enactment of this Act."[26]

A similar story of congressional hardball occurred in 1992. In the midst of his reelection campaign, President George H. W. Bush decided to put Congress on the defensive by sending up a list of programs to be eliminated. He would get credit for being a "fiscal guardian." If Congress didn't approve his proposals, it would be condemned for wasteful spending. He planned to submit new lists each month. To strengthen his position, Bush identified a number of seemingly frivolous programs, including asparagus research, celery research, prickly pear research, Vidalia onion storage, and manure disposal. His total came to $7.9 billion.

Senator Byrd was more than ready to play this game. He produced an even larger package of cuts: ($8.2 billion), but his list would demonstrate that there "is plenty of 'pork' . . . at the other end of Pennsylvania Avenue."[27] The congressional substitute included plans by the executive branch to study the significance of holism in German-speaking society and a $94,000 study of why people feared going to the dentist. To Byrd the reason was obvious: "Any child who has to go to the dentist will tell you why he fears the dentist. It hurts."[28] Other executive branch programs to be terminated by the congressional list: research grants for monogamy and aggression in fish in Nicaragua, the well-being of middle-class lawyers, sexual mimicry of swallowtail butterflies, and song production in freely behaving birds. Bush was in a spot. Having gone public on his pledge to cut federal spending, he had little choice but to sign the congressional substitute. He did not send up future lists.[29]

Constitutional Checks

The initiatives on SDI testing, Rehnquist's nomination, and Bush's rescission strategy came from lawmakers determined to protect institutional interests. They did what Madison hoped for in Federalist No. 51, using "personal motives to resist encroachments of the others." When Tom Foley (D-WA) became a member of the House of Representatives in 1965, he had no idea he would rise in the ranks to become Speaker in 1989. What he did know, from the start, was the importance of thinking for himself. Lawmakers had to understand that they represented a separate branch with separate duties: "The members of Congress must be independent. The Congress is designed to be a separate entity from the president, not to be the instrument of presidential power, but to be a separate check and balance to the president, not to oppose him all the time, not to support him all the time, but to have a different viewpoint."[30]

Foley also understood that when lawmakers represent their states and districts they must remain free to exercise independent judgment, even when they disappoint some constituents. Members of Congress have a representative function but not to the point of trying at every step to simply reflect what local public polls indicate. Foley remarked: "Throughout my career one of my own unspoken standards was that if I didn't take at least one vote a term that jeopardized my job, then I was maybe going down a slippery slope."[31]

The search for common ground by lawmakers is a necessary part of the political process. Surrendering institutional interests to other branches is not. An active system of checks and balances is not only consistent with constitutional principles but produces better policies and smarter, safer politics. That lesson, driven home many times, must be rediscovered and practiced regularly.

NOTES

Preface

1. Paul J. Quirk and Sarah A. Binder, eds., *The Legislative Branch* (New York: Oxford University Press, 2005), xx, 525.

2. Julian E. Zelizer, ed., *The American Congress: The Building of Democracy* (Boston: Houghton Mifflin, 2004), xiv.

Chapter I

1. Louis Fisher, *In the Name of National Security: Unchecked Presidential Power and the Reynolds Case* (Lawrence: University Press of Kansas, 2006), 4–5.

2. John Nevill Figgis, *The Theory of the Divine Right of Kings* (Cambridge, UK: At the University Press, 1896). His second edition was published in 1914 under the title *The Divine Right of Kings* and reprinted in 1994 as a paperback by Thoemmes Press.

3. Fritz Kern, *Kingship and Law in the Middle Ages*, translated by S. B. Chrimes (New York: Harper Torchbook, 1970), 140.

4. Stephen D. White, *Sir Edward Cook and "the Grievances of the Commonwealth," 1621–1628* (Chapel Hill: University of North Carolina Press, 1979).

5. Carl L. Becker, *The Declaration of Independence* (New York: Vintage Books, 1959), 51.

6. Among the many fine studies of political reforms in England and America, see Carl Ubbelohde, *The American Colonies and the British Empire, 1607–1763* (New York: Thomas Y. Crowell, 1968); Edmund S.

Morgan, *Inventing the People: The Rise of Popular Sovereignty in England and America* (New York: Norton, 1988); and Alan Taylor, *American Colonies: The Settling of North America* (New York: Penguin, 2001).

7. Edmund S. Morgan and Helen M. Morgan, *The Stamp Act Crisis: Prologue to Revolution* (Chapel Hill: University of North Carolina Press, 1995 ed.), 95. This is an excellent study of the problems of administering this law and the growing spirit of self-government and independence in America.

8. Charles Andrews, *The Colonial Background of the American Revolution* (New Haven, CT: Yale University Press, 1961 ed.), 63.

9. Thomas Paine, *Common Sense and Other Political Writings* (New York: The Liberal Arts Press, 1953), 32 (italics in original).

10. Francis Wharton, *The Revolutionary Correspondence of the United States* (Washington, DC: Government Printing Office, 1889), vol. 1, 663. For additional details on the influence of Montesquieu and other writers and the creation of boards, single executives, and a separate court by the Continental Congress, see Louis Fisher, *President and Congress: Power and Policy* (New York: Free Press, 1972), 1–17, 241–270, 273–278, 329–334.

11. M. J. C. Vile, *Constitutionalism and the Separation of Powers* (Oxford: Oxford University Press, 1967), 153.

12. *Annals of Congress*, vol. 1, 453 (June 8, 1789).

13. George Washington, *The Writings of George Washington*, vol. 1, ed. John C. Fitzpatrick (Washington, DC: Government Printing Office), 506 (emphasis in original). For background on this issue, see Louis Fisher, *The Constitution and 9/11: Recurring Threats to America's Freedoms* (Lawrence: University Press of Kansas, 2008), 60–68; Robert M. Chesney, "Democratic-Republican Societies, Subversion, and the Limits of Legitimate Dissent in the Early Republic," *North Carolina Law Review*, vol. 82, 1525 (2004); and Eugene Perry Link, *Democratic-Republican Societies, 1790–1800* (New York: Columbia University Press, 1942). For a collection of documents on these political clubs, see Philip S. Foner, ed., *The Democratic-Republican Societies, 1790–1800* (Westport, CT: Greenwood, 1976).

14. Washington, *The Writings of George Washington*, vol. 33, 523.

15. Letter of Edmund Randolph to George Washington, October 11, 1794, George Washington Papers, Series 4, Reel 106, Library of Congress Manuscript Division.

16. Washington, *The Writings of George Washington*, vol. 34, 37.

17. *Annals of Congress*, 3d Cong., 1–2 Sess. 901 (1794).

18. Ibid., 910.

19. Ibid., 913–914.

20. Ibid., 934.

21. Ibid.

22. Madison's essay is reprinted in James Madison, *The Writings of James Madison*, ed. Gaillard Hunt, vol. 6, 101–103.

23. Jefferson, *The Writings of Thomas Jefferson*, vol. 3, 263.

24. Benedict de Spinoza, *A Theological-Political Treatise* (Mineola, NY: Dover Publications, 2004), 257.

25. *Whitney v. California*, 274 U.S. 357, 375 (1927) (Brandeis, J., concurring).

26. Ibid.

27. James Morton Smith, *Freedom's Fetters: The Alien and Sedition Laws and American Civil Liberties* (Ithaca, NY: Cornell University Press, 1956), 15.

28. H. Rept. No. 86, 26th Cong., 1st Sess. (1840), 2; 6 Stat. 802, ch. 45 (1840).

29. Paul Douglas Newman, *Fries's Rebellion: The Enduring Struggle for the American Revolution* (Philadelphia: University of Pennsylvania Press, 2004).

30. *Whitney v. California*, 375–376.

31. *Congressional Globe*, 42d Cong., 2d Sess., 1287 (February 29, 1872).

32. "Iran-Contra Investigation," joint hearings before the Senate Select Committee on Secret Military Assistance to Iran and the Nicaraguan Opposition and the House Select Committee to Investigate Covert Arms Transactions with Iran, 100th Cong., 1st Sess., vol. 100–107 (Part II), 45–46.

33. Glenn Kessler, "Hagel Defends Criticism of Iraq Policy," *Washington Post*, November 16, 2005, A6 (emphasis added).

34. Geoffrey R. Stone, *Perilous Times: Free Speech in Wartime* (New York: Norton, 2004), 211.

35. Fisher, *The Constitution and 9/11*, 131–138.

36. *Schenck v. United States,* 249 U.S. 47, 52 (1919).

Chapter 2

1. *United States v. Lopez,* 514 U.S. 549, 552 (1995); *City of Boerne v. Flores,* 521 U.S 507, 516 (1997).

2. *Annals of Congress,* vol. 1, 761 (August 18, 1789).

3. Steven G. Calabresi and Christopher S. Yoo, *The Unitary Executive: Presidential Power from Washington to Bush* (New Haven, CT: Yale University Press, 2008), 4.

4. 17 U.S. (4 Wheat.) 315, 420 (1819).

5. James D. Richardson, ed., *A Compilation of the Messages and Papers of the Presidents,* 20 vols. (New York: Bureau of National Literature, 1897–1925), vol. 1, 416 (October 27, 1807) (hereafter "Richardson").

6. Thomas Jefferson, *The Writings of Thomas Jefferson,* ed. H. A. Washington (9 vols., New York: H. W. Derby, 1861), vol. 5, 542–545.

7. Richardson, vol. 7, 3225.

8. *The Prize Cases*, 67 U.S. 635, 660 (emphasis in original). Justice Grier's comment appears on 668.

9. *United States v. Curtiss-Wright,* 299 U.S. 304, 319 (1936).

10. Ibid.

11. Quoted in Louis Fisher, *The Constitution and 9/11: Recurring Threats to America's Freedoms* (Lawrence: University Press of Kansas, 2008), 294.

12. In 2002 the FISA Court of Review stated: "We take it for granted that the President does have that authority [to conduct warrantless searches to obtain foreign intelligence information] and, assuming that is so, FISA could not encroach on the President's constitutional power." *In re Sealed Case*, 310 F.3d 717, 742 (Foreign Int.Surv.Ct. Rev. 2002). "Taking it for granted" and "assuming that is so" falls short of legal analysis. Moreover, the FISA Court is a secret court without any adversary process for determining the truth or settling constitutional questions.

13. *Talbot v. Seeman,* 5 U.S. 1, 28 (1801); see also *Bas v. Tingy*, 4 U.S. 37 (1800).

14. *Little v. Barreme*, 6 U.S. (2 Cr.) 169, 179 (1804). For further analysis of the "sole organ" doctrine, see Louis Fisher, "Presidential Inherent Power: The 'Sole Organ Doctrine,'" *Presidential Studies Quarterly*, vol. 37, no. 1, 139–152 (March 2007).

15. U.S. Congress, H. Doc. No. 534 (part 1), 82d Cong., 2d Sess., 371–372 (1952).

16. *Youngstown Sheet & Tube Co. v. Sawyer*, 103 F. Supp. 569 (D.D.C. 1952), aff'd 343 U.S. 579 (1952).

17. Ibid.

18. Ibid. See Maeva Marcus, *Truman and the* Steel Seizure Case: *The Limits of Presidential Power* (Durham, NC: Duke University Press, 1994).

19. For impoundment, see James P. Pfiffner, *President, the Budget and Congress: Impoundment and the 1974 Budget Act* (Boulder, CO: West-

view Press, 1979); and Louis Fisher, *Presidential Spending Power* (Princeton, NJ: Princeton University Press, 1975), 147–201. For litigation striking down domestic surveillance, see *United States v. United States District Court*, 407 U.S. 297 (1972); and Fisher, *The Constitution and 9/11*, 285–290.

20. *United States v. United States District Court for the Eastern District of Michigan*, 444 F.2d 651, 665 (6th Cir. 1971).

21. Brief for Respondents, *Hamdan v. Rumsfeld*, on writ of certiorari to the United States Court of Appeals for the District of Columbia Circuit, U.S. Supreme Court, No. 05-184, February 2006, 9.

22. *Hamdan v. Rumsfeld*, 548 U.S. 557 (2006); Military Commissions Act of 2006, P.L. 109–366, 120 Stat. 2600.

23. Brief for Respondents-Appellants, *Hamdi v. Rumsfeld*, No. 02–6895 (4th Cir. 2002), 14.

24. *Hamdi v. Rumsfeld*, 542 U.S. 507, 535–536 (2004).

25. *Rasul v. Bush*, 542 U.S. 466 (2004).

26. *Boumediene v. Bush*, 553 U.S. ___ (2008).

27. Fisher, *The Constitution and 9/11*, 285–320.

28. Henry Steele Commager, "Presidential Power: The Issue Analyzed," *New York Times Magazine* (January 14, 1951): 11. See also his article "Does the President Have Too Much Power?" *New York Times Magazine* (April 1, 1951): 15.

29. Arthur M. Schlesinger Jr., "Presidential Powers: Taft Statement on Troops Opposed, Actions of Past Precedents Cited," *New York Times,* January 9, 1951, 28.

30. Ibid.

31. Edward S. Corwin, "The President's Power," *New Republic,* January 29, 1951, 15.

32. Arthur M. Schlesinger Jr., *The Imperial Presidency* (Boston: Houghton Mifflin, 1973), ix.

33. Richard E. Neustadt, *Presidential Power* (New York: Signet, 1964), 174.

34. For further details on Commager, Schlesinger, and Neustadt, see Louis Fisher, "Scholarly Support for Presidential Wars," *Presidential Studies Quarterly*, vol. 35, no. 3 (September 2005), 590–607.

35. Friedrich A. Hayek, "Why I Am Not a Conservative," in *What Is Conservatism?* ed. Frank S. Meyers (New York: Holt, Rinehart and Winston, 1964), 100.

36. James Burnham, *Congress and the American Tradition* (Chicago: Regnery, 1959), 92.

37. Ibid., 184.

38. Ibid., 344.

39. Willmoore Kendall, "The Two Majorities," *Midwest Journal of Political Science*, vol. 4 (1960), 317–345.

40. Alfred de Grazia, *Republic in Crisis: Congress Against the Executive Force* (New York: Federal Legal Publications, 1965), 72.

41. Ibid.

42. Ronald C. Moe, ed., *Congress and the President: Allies and Adversaries* (Pacific Palisades, CA: Goodyear, 1971), 3.

43. John Hart, "Presidential Power Revisited," *Political Studies*, vol. 25 (1977), 48–61; David Gray Adler, "Textbooks and the President's Constitutional Powers," *Presidential Studies Quarterly*, vol. 35 (2005), 376–388.

44. Norman Podhoretz, "Making the World Safe for Communism," *Commentary*, April 1976, 35.

45. Joseph M. Bessette and Jeffrey Tulis, eds., *The Presidency in the Constitutional Order* (Baton Rouge: Louisiana State University Press, 1981); see also Joseph M. Bessette, *The Mild Voice of Reason: Deliberative Democracy and American National Government* (Chicago: University Press of Chicago, 1994).

46. Mickey Edwards, *Reclaiming Conservatism* (New York: Oxford University Press, 2008), 185.

47. Max Farrand, ed., *The Records of the Federal Convention of 1787* (New Haven, CT: Yale University Press, 1937), vol. 2, 318.

48. Ibid.

49. John C. Yoo, "The Continuation of Politics by Other Means: The Original Understanding of War Powers," *California Law Review*, vol. 84, no. 2 (March 1996), 167–305. Many of these arguments appear in Yoo's book, *The Powers of War and Peace: The Constitution and Foreign Affairs After 9/11* (Chicago: University of Chicago Press, 2005).

50. *United States v. Smith*, 27 Fed. Cas. 1192 (C.C.N.Y. 1806) (No. 16, 342).

51. For some evaluations of John Yoo's scholarship, see Louis Fisher, "Unchecked Presidential Wars," *University of Pennsylvania Law Review*, vol. 148 (2000), 1637–1672; David Cole, "What Bush Wants to Hear," *New York Review of Books*, November 17, 2005, 8–12; Gordon Silverstein, "All Power to the President," *The American Prospect*, vol. 17, no. 3 (March 2006), 1–6; David Luban, "The Defense of Torture," *New York Review of Books*, March 15, 2007, 37–40; Robert F. Turner, "An Insider's Look at the War on Terrorism," *Cornell Law Review*, vol. 93 (2008), 471–500; Stuart Streichler, "Mad About Yoo, or, Why Worry About the Next Unconstitutional War?" *Journal of Law & Politics*, vol. 24 (2008), 93–128.

52. *Congressional Record*, vol. 55, 363 (1917).

53. Louis Fisher, *Presidential War Power* (Lawrence: University Press of Kansas, 2d ed., 2004), 133–135.

54. Singer's remarks appear in David W. Clinton, *The Two Faces of National Interest* (Baton Rouge: Louisiana State University Press, 1994), x.

55. George S. Edwards III, "Congress and National Strategy: The Appropriate Role?" in *U.S. National Security Strategy for the 1990s*, ed. Daniel J. Kaufman, David S. Clark, and Kevin P. Sheehan (Baltimore, MD: Johns Hopkins University Press, 1991), 82.

56. Alexander DeConde, *Presidential Machismo: Executive Authority, Military Intervention, and Foreign Relations* (Boston: Northeastern University Press, 2000), 294.

57. Richard M. Pious, "Why Do Presidents Fail?," *Presidential Studies Quarterly*, vol. 32 (2002), 727.

58. Richard M. Pious, *Why Presidents Fail* (Lanham, MD: Rowman and Littlefield, 2008), 247.

59. James P. Pfiffner, *The Character Factor: How We Judge America's Presidents* (College Station: Texas A&M University Press, 2004); Eric Alterman, *Why Presidents Lie: A History of Official Deception and Its Consequences* (New York: Viking, 2004). For a string of false and deceptive claims about weapons of mass destruction held by Iraq in 2002, see Louis Fisher, "Justifying War Against Iraq," in *Rivals for Power: Presidential-Congressional Relations*, ed. James A. Thurber (Lanham, MD: Rowman and Littlefield, 2006), 289–313.

60. E.g., Gene Healy, *The Cult of the Presidency: America's Dangerous Devotion to Executive Power* (Washington, DC: Cato Institute, 2008); Dana D. Nelson, *Bad for Democracy: How the Presidency Undermines the Power of the People* (Minneapolis: University of Minnesota Press, 2008); James P. Pfiffner, *Power Play: The Bush Presidency and the Constitution* (Washington, DC: Brookings Institution Press, 2008); Matthew Crenson and Benjamin Ginsberg, *Presidential Power: Unchecked and Unbalanced* (New York: W. W. Norton, 2007); Charlie Savage, *Takeover: The Return of the Imperial Presidency and the Subversion of American Democracy* (New York: Little, Brown, 2007); Andrew Rudalevige, *The New Imperial Presidency: Renewing Presidential Power After Watergate* (Ann Arbor: University of Michigan Press, 2005).

Chapter 3

1. *Brown v. Allen,* 344 U.S. 443, 540 (1953) (Jackson, J., concurring).

2. *United States v. Lovett,* 328 U.S. 303 (1946).

3. *Marbury v. Madison,* 5 U.S. (1 Cr.) 137 (1803).

4. *Hylton v. United States,* 3 Dall. 171, 175 (1796), emphasis in original.

5. *Hollingsworth v. Virginia,* 3 Dall. 378 (1798).

6. *Calder v. Bull,* 3 Dall. 386, 399 (1798) (Iredell, J., concurring).

7. *Marbury v. Madison,* 177.

8. Louis Fisher and Katy J. Harriger, *American Constitutional Law,* 8th ed. (Durham, NC: Carolina Academic Press, 2009), 43.

9. David P. Currie, *The Constitution in Congress* (Chicago: University of Chicago Press, 1997), 296.

10. Francis Wharton, *State Trials of the United States During the Administration of Washington and Adams* (Philadelphia: Carey and Hart, 1849), 84–85, 88; Henfield's Case, 11 F. Cas. 1099 (C.C. Pa. 1793) (No. 6,360).

11. *United States v. Hudson and Goodwin,* 11 U.S. (7 Cr.) 32 (1812); *United States v. Coolidge,* 14 U.S. (1 Wheat.) 415 (1816); Leonard W. Levy, *Jefferson and Civil Liberties: The Darker Side* (New York: Quadrangle, 1973), chap. 3; Herbert A. Johnson, *History of the Supreme Court of the United States: Foundations of Power: John Marshall, 1801–1815* (New York: Macmillan, 1981), 633–646; Richard Buel Jr., *America on the Brink: How the Political Struggle over the War of 1812 Almost Destroyed the Young Republic* (New York: Palgrave Macmillan, 2005), 147, 162, 196.

12. *Pennsylvania v. Wheeling &c. Bridge Co.,* 54 U.S. (13 How.) 518 (1852); 10 Stat. 110, 112, sec. 6 (1852); *Pennsylvania v. Wheeling and Belmont Bridge Co.,* 59 U.S. (18 How.) 421 (1856). See also *Prudential Ins. Co. v. Benjamin,* 326 U.S. 408, 425 (1946); *United States v. Lopez,* 514 U.S. 549, 580 (1995).

13. Harold M. Hyman, *A More Perfect Union* (Boston: Houghton Mifflin, 1975), 6.

14. *Dred Scott v. Sandford,* 60 U.S. (19 How.) 393 (1857).

15. Quoted in Stanley I. Kutner, *The* Dred Scott *Decision: Law or Politics?* (Boston: Houghton Mifflin, 1967), 47.

16. *Political Debates Between Abraham Lincoln and Stephen A. Douglas* (Cleveland, OH: The Burrows Brothers Co., 1894), 70–71, 76–77, 78–79.

17. *Prudential Ins. Co. v. Benjamin,* 328 U.S. 408, 415 (1946).

18. Owen J. Roberts, *The Court and the Constitution* (Cambridge, MA: Harvard University Press, 1951), 61.

19. Robert H. Jackson, "Maintaining Our Freedoms: The Role of the Judiciary," *Vital Speeches*, no. 24, vol. XIX, October 1, 1951, 761.

20. *Hepburn v. Griswold,* 8 Wall. (75 U.S.) 603 (1870).

21. *Legal Tender Cases,* 12 Wall. (79 U.S.) 457 (1871).

22. *United States v. Cruikshank,* 92 U.S. (2 Otto.) 542, 550 (1876).

23. *Leisy v. Hardin,* 135 U.S. 100 (1890).

24. Quoted in Fisher and Harriger, *American Constitutional Law*, 323.

25. *In re Rahrer,* 140 U.S. 545 (1891).

26. *Hylton v. United States*, 3 Dall. at 171.

27. *Veazie Bank v. Fenno,* 75 U.S. (8 Wall.) 533 (1869).

28. *Springer v. United States,* 102 U.S. 586 (1881).

29. Ibid., 594.

30. *Pollock v. Farmers' Loan & Trust Co.,* 157 U.S. 429 (1895).

31. Ibid., 532.

32. Ibid., 607.

33. Charles Evans Hughes, *The Supreme Court of the United States* (New York: Columbia University Press, 1928), 54.

34. *Hammer v. Dagenhart,* 247 U.S. 251 (1918).

35. *Congressional Record*, vol. 56, 7433 (1918).

36. "Brief on Behalf of Appellants and Plaintiff in Error," *J. W. Bailey and J. W. Bailey, Collector of Internal Revenue for the District of North Carolina v. Drexel Furniture Co.*, in *Landmark Briefs and Arguments of the Supreme Court of the United States: Constitutional Law* (Arlington, VA: University Publications of America, 1975), 59.

37. *Bailey v. Drexel Furniture Co.,* 259 U.S. 20 (1922).

38. Ibid., 38.

39. Fisher and Harriger, *American Constitutional Law*, 442–445.

40. *United States v. Darby,* 312 U.S. 100 (1941).

41. Ibid., 116–117.

42. Jonathan Elliot, ed., *The Debates in the Several State Conventions on the Adoption of the Federal Constitution*, vol. 3 (Philadelphia, PA: Lippincott, 1937), 459.

43. Louis Fisher, "Confidential Spending and Government Accountability," *George Washington Law Review*, vol. 47 (1979), 347.

44. *United States v. Richardson,* 418 U.S. 166, 179 (1974).

45. Ibid., 200–201.

46. "Making Connections with Dots to Decipher U.S. Spy Spending," *Washington Post*, March 12, 1996, A11.

47. Louis Fisher, *Constitutional Conflicts Between Congress and the President* (Lawrence, KS: University Press of Kansas, 2007), 213–214.

48. Mark Mazzetti, "$43.5 Billion Spying Budget for Year, Not Including Military," *New York Times*, October 31, 2007, A16; Walter Pincus, "2007 Spying Said to Cost $50 Billion," *Washington Post*, October 30, 2007, A4.

49. Louis Fisher, *The Politics of Executive Privilege* (Durham, NC: Carolina Academic Press, 2004), 254–255.

50. *Opinions of the Attorney General*, vol. 6 (1854), 680.

51. For details on the experience with the legislative veto, see Fisher, *Constitutional Conflicts Between Congress and the President*, 137–154.

52. *INS v. Chadha,* 462 U.S. 919 (1983).

53. Louis Fisher, "Congress Can't Lose on Its Veto Power," *Washington Post*, February 21, 1982, D1, D5.

54. *Chadha*, 462 U.S. at 944.

55. William Howard Taft, "Criticisms of the Federal Judiciary," *American Law Review*, vol. 29 (1895), 643.

56. Sandra Day O'Connor, *The Majesty of the Law: Reflections of a Supreme Court Justice* (New York: Random House, 2003), 44, 45.

Chapter 4

1. *Annals of Congress*, vol. 1, 439 (1789).

2. *Annals of Congress*, 5th Cong., 2d and 3d Sessions, vol. 9 (1798), 2152.

3. *The Writings of Thomas Jefferson*, memorial ed., vol. 10 (Washington, DC: Thomas Jefferson Memorial Association, 1903–1904), 61.

4. Henry W. Edgerton, "The Incidence of Judicial Control over Congress," *Cornell Law Quarterly*, vol. 22 (1937), 299.

5. S. Rept. No. 711, 75th Cong., 1st Session (1937), 3, 19, 20, 23.

6. *United States v. Carolene Products Co.*, 304 U.S. 144, 152–153 n.4 (1938).

7. Leslie Friedman Goldstein, "The ERA and the U.S. Supreme Court," *Research in Law and Policy Studies*, vol. 1 (1987), 154–155.

8. John J. Dinan, *Keeping the People's Liberties: Legislators, Citizens, and Judges as Guardians of Rights* (Lawrence: University Press of Kansas, 1998). See also Larry D. Kramer, *The People Themselves: Popular Constitutionalism and Judicial Review* (New York: Oxford University Press,

2004) and Kramer, *"Here, the People Rule": A Constitutional Populist Manifesto* (Cambridge, MA: Harvard University Press, 1994).

9. Harry Kalven Jr. and Hans Zeisel, *The American Jury* (Boston: Little, Brown, 1966), 319.

10. *Webb, Auditor & Co. v. Bird*, 6 Ind. 11, 15 (1854); *Carpenter & Sprague v. Dane County*, 9 Wis. 274, 276 (1859); *Gideon v. Wainwright*, 372 U.S. 335 (1963).

11. For recognition of the rights of conscientious objectors by communities and legislatures, see Louis Fisher, *Religious Liberty in America: Political Safeguards* (Lawrence: University Press of Kansas, 2002), 82–104.

12. Edward Needles Wright, *Conscientious Objectors in the Civil War* (Philadelphia: University of Pennsylvania Press, 1931), 70–71.

13. Ibid., 72.

14. 13 Stat. 6, 9 (1864).

15. 40 Stat. 40, 68 (1917); Executive Order 2823 (March 20, 1918).

16. 54 Stat. 885, 889 (1940).

17. *Congressional Record*, 43d Cong., 2d Session, vol. 3, 940 (1875).

18. *Civil Rights Cases,* 109 U.S. 3 (1883).

19. Ibid., 59–60.

20. *In re Bradwell*, 55 Ill. 535, 542 (1869).

21. Ibid., 540.

22. Illinois Laws, 1871–1872, 578.

23. 16 Wall. (83 U.S.) 130, 139 (1873).

24. Ibid., 141–142.

25. *Congressional Record*, vol. 7, 1235 (1878).

26. *Congressional Record*, vol. 8, 1084 (1879).

27. Ibid.

28. Edward T. James, ed., *Notable American Women, 1607–1950* (Cambridge, MA: Harvard University Press, 1971), 414.

29. *Reed v. Reed,* 404 U.S. 71 (1971).

30. *Goeseart v. Cleary,* 335 U.S. 464 (1948).

31. Ibid., 465.

32. *Hoyt v. Florida,* 368 U.S. 57, 62 (1961).

33. John D. Johnston Jr. and Charles L. Knapp, "Sex Discrimination by Law: A Study in Judicial Perspective," *New York University Law Review*, vol. 46 (1971), 676.

34. *Congressional Record*, 91st Cong., 2d Sess., vol. 117, 35323 (1971).

35. *Minersville School District v. Gobitis,* 310 U.S. 586 (1940).

36. Cited in *Minersville School District v. Gobitis*, 21 F. Supp. 581, 584 (E.D. Pa. 1937).

37. H. N. Hirsch, *The Enigma of Felix Frankfurter* (New York: Basic Books, 1981), 152.

38. Fisher, *Religious Liberty in America,* 109.

39. *Jones v. Opelika,* 316 U.S. 584 (1942).

40. Fisher, *Religious Liberty in America*, 112–113; 46 Stat. 380, sec. 7 (1942).

41. *West Virginia State Board of Education v. Barnette,* 319 U.S. 624, 638 (1943).

42. E.g., *Cantwell v. Connecticut*, 310 U.S. 296 (1940) (upholding the right of a Jehovah's Witness to solicit money and sell books); *Largent v. Texas*, 318 U.S. 418 (1943) (striking down an ordinance that required a permit to solicit orders and sell books); and *Murdoch v. Pennsylvania*, 319 U.S. 105 (1943) (striking down a license tax applied to Jehovah's Witnesses who engaged in missionary evangelism).

43. *Goldman v. Secretary of Defense*, 530 F. Supp. 12, 15, 16 (D.D.C. 1981); *Bitterman v. Secretary of Defense*, 553 F. Supp. 719, 725 (D.D.C. 1982).

44. *Goldman v. Weinberger,* 475 U.S. 503 (1986).

45. Ibid., 514.

46. Ibid., 523, 524.

47. *Congressional Record*, 99th Cong., 2d Sess., vol. 132, 19803 (1986).

48. *Brown v. Board of Education,* 347 U.S. 483 (1954).

49. *Plessy v. Ferguson,* 163 U.S. 537 (1896).

50. For divisions within the Court prior to *Brown*, see the box in Fisher and Harriger, *American Constitutional Law*, 771.

51. *Brown v. Board of Education*, 357 U.S. 483, 495 (1954).

52. *Brown v. Board of Education*, 349 U.S. 294, 298 (1955).

53. Ibid., 299.

54. Ibid., 300.

55. *Griffin v. School Bd.*, 377 U.S. 218, 229 (1964) (emphasis in original).

56. *United States v. Jefferson County Board of Education*, 372 F.2d 836, 837 (5th Cir. 1966) (emphasis in original).

57. *Heart of Atlanta Motel v. United States*, 379 U.S. 241 (1964); *Katzenbach v. McClung*, 379 U.S. 294 (1964).

58. *Naim v. Naim*, 87 S.E.2d 749, 756 (Va. 1955).

59. *Naim v. Naim*, 350 U.S. 891 (1955).

60. *Naim v. Naim*, 350 U.S. 985 (1956).

61. *Loving v. Virginia,* 388 U.S. 1 (1967).

62. Earl Warren, "The Bill of Rights and the Military," *New York University Law Review*, vol. 37 (1962), 181.

Chapter 5

1. *Congressional Record*, vol. 79, 2014 (1935).

2. *Congressional Digest*, vol. xvi, 172 (June-July 1937).

3. *Congressional Record*, vol. 84, 2854 (1939).

4. Louis Fisher, *Presidential Spending Power* (Princeton, NJ: Princeton University Press, 1975), 214.

5. *Public Papers and Addresses of Franklin D. Roosevelt*, vol. 11, 364–365 (New York: Random House, 1950).

6. Woodrow Wilson, *The Papers of Woodrow Wilson*, ed. Arthur S. Link (Princeton, NJ: Princeton University Press), vol. 63, 451, and vol. 64, 47, 51; Louis Fisher, *Presidential War Power* (Lawrence: University Press of Kansas, 2d ed., 2004), 81–83.

7. *Congressional Record*, vol. 91, 8185 (1945).

8. Fisher, *Presidential War Power*, 84–95.

9. *Public Papers of the Presidents* (Washington, DC: Government Printing Office), vol. 1950, 504.

10. Fisher, *Presidential War Power*, 169–172, 180–192.

11. Ibid., 105–115.

12. "Background Information on the Use of United States Armed Forces in Foreign Countries," printed for the use of the House Committee on Foreign Affairs, 82d Cong., 1st Sess. (Comm. Print, 1951), 1.

13. H. Doc. No. 443, 84th Cong., 2d Sess. (1956), viii.

14. Dwight D. Eisenhower, *Waging Peace* (Garden City, NY: Doubleday, 1965), 179.

15. J. William Fulbright, "American Foreign Policy in the Twentieth Century under an Eighteenth-Century Constitution," *Cornell Law Quarterly* 47 (1961): 2.

16. U.S. Commitments to Foreign Powers," hearings before the Senate Foreign Relations Committee, 90th Cong., 1st Session (1967), 3.

17. S. Rept. No. 129, 91st Cong., 1st Session (1969), 8.

18. Ibid., 16.

19. Ibid., 23 (emphasis in original).

20. Fisher, *Presidential War Power*, 145.

21. Ibid., 148.

22. Louis Fisher, "The Baker-Christopher War Power Commission," *Presidential Studies Quarterly*, vol. 39, no. 1 (March 2009), 128–140.

23. *Train v. City of New York,* 420 U.S. 35 (1975).

24. H. Rept. No. 147, 93d Cong., 1st Session (1973), 1.

25. *Congressional Record*, vol. 125, 9028 (1979).

26. Louis Fisher, *The Politics of Shared Power: Congress and the Executive*, 4th ed. (College Station, Texas A&M University Press, 1998), 234.

27. David A. Stockman, *The Triumph of Politics* (New York: Harper and Row, 1986), 159.

28. Ibid., 91.

29. Allen Schick, *The Capacity to Budget* (Washington, DC: Urban Institute Press, 1990), 204.

30. *Bowsher v. Synar,* 478 U.S. 714 (1986).

31. Fisher, *The Politics of Shared Power*, 240 (Table 7-3).

32. "Budget Process Reform," hearing before the House Committee on the Budget, 101st Cong., 2d Session (1990), 20–21.

33. *Clinton v. City of New York,* 524 U.S. 417 (1998).

34. Mickey Edwards, *Reclaiming Conservatism* (New York: Oxford University Press, 2008), 174.

35. *Public Papers of the Presidents* (Washington, DC: Government Printing Office, 1984), 1228.

36. *Congressional Record*, vol. 141, 2361 (1995), 135.

Chapter 6

1. Lee Hamilton, *How Congress Works and Why You Should Care* (Bloomington: Indiana University Press, 2004), 23. A very thoughtful analysis of the many virtues of Congress and a frank, informed assessment of its weaknesses.

2. Thomas E. Mann and Norman J. Ornstein, *The Broken Branch: How Congress Is Failing America and How to Get It Back on Track* (New York: Oxford University Press, 2006), 215.

3. *Whitney v. California*, 274 U.S. 357, 375 (1927) (Brandeis, J., concurring).

4. Specific examples of individuals who made a difference are listed in Lee Hamilton's book, 138–140.

5. Frederick A. O. Schwarz Jr. and Aziz S. Huq, *Unchecked and Unbalanced: Presidential Power in a Time of Terror* (New York: New Press, 2007), 204.

6. Mann and Ornstein, *The Broken Branch,* xi.

7. *Congressional Quarterly Weekly Report*, March 30, 2009, 707.

8. Newt Gingrich, *Lessons Learned the Hard Way* (New York: HarperCollins, 1998), 144–147, 149–152.

9. Jim Wright, *Balance of Power: Presidents and Congress from the Era of McCarthy to the Age of Gingrich* (Atlanta, GA: Turner, 1996), 382.

10. Tip O'Neill, *Man of the House: The Life and Political Memoirs of Speaker Tip O'Neill* (New York: Random House, 1987), 190.

11. Ibid., 194–195.

12. Carl Albert, *Little Giant: The Life and Times of Speaker Carl Albert* (Norman: University of Oklahoma Press, 1990), 165.

13. Ibid., 294–301.

14. *Bush v. Gore,* 531 U.S. 98 (2000).

15. The literature on *Bush* v. *Gore* is vast, but a good analysis appears in Charles L. Zelden, Bush v. Gore: *Exposing the Hidden Crisis in American Democracy* (Lawrence: University Press of Kansas, 2008).

16. Gore's concession speech of December 13, 2000, http://abcnews.go.com/print?id=122220.

17. Ibid.

18. *Congressional Record*, vol. 155, S12 (daily ed. January 6, 2009).

19. *Buckley v. Valeo,* 424 U.S. 1 (1976).

20. Legistorm, "About Congressional Staff Salaries," http://www.legistorm.com/salaries/aboutcs.html, accessed June 27, 2009.

21. Other possible reforms are explored in Susan Crabtree, "Obey Tackles Earmarks, but Colleagues Skeptical," *The Hill*, June 18, 2009, 6.

22. Christopher Drew, "Work Halted on Helicopter for President," *New York Times*, May 16, 2009, B1.

23. Christopher Drew, "$296 Billion in Overruns in U.S. Weapons Programs," *New York Times*, March 31, 2009, B8.

24. Nick Schwellenbach, "Fraud Cases Fell While Pentagon Contracts Surged," April 1, 2009, available at Center for Public Integrity website, http:www.publicintegrity.org/articles/entry/1243, accessed June 27, 2009.

25. Louis Fisher, *The Politics of Executive Privilege* (Durham, NC: Carolina Academic Press, 2004), 76–77.

26. 101 Stat. 1057, sec. 226 (1987).

27. *Congressional Record*, vol. 138, 6807 (1992).

28. "House Rearranges Bush's Budget Cuts," *Washington Post*, May 8, 1992, A8.

29. Louis Fisher, *Congressional Abdication on War and Spending* (College Station: Texas A&M University Press, 2000), 145–146.

30. Tom Foley, *Honor in the House* (Pullman: Washington State University Press, 1999), 32–33.

31. Ibid., 224, 243.

Index

ABOUT THE AUTHOR

Louis Fisher is a specialist in constitutional law at the Law Library of the Library of Congress, after working with the Congressional Research Service from 1970 to March 2006. The views expressed in this book are personal, not institutional. During his service with CRS, Fisher was research director of the House Iran-Contra Committee in 1987, writing major sections of the final report. He is the author of nineteen books, including *The Constitution and 9/11: Recurring Threats to America's Freedoms* (2008), *In the Name of National Security: Unchecked Presidential Power and the Reynolds Case* (2006), *Military Tribunals and Presidential Power: American Revolution to the War on Terrorism* (2005), *The Politics of Executive Privilege* (2004), *Presidential War Power* (2d ed. 2004), *Constitutional Conflicts between Congress and the President* (5th ed. 2007), and *American Constitutional Law* (with Katy J. Harriger, 8th ed., 2009). He has received the Dartmouth Book Award, the Neustadt Book Award, and has twice received the Louis Brownlow Book Award.

He received his doctorate in political science from the New School for Social Research (1967) and has taught at Queens College, Georgetown University, American University, Catholic University, Indiana University, Johns Hopkins University, and the law schools of William and Mary and Catholic University. He has testified before congressional committees on such issues as state secrets, war powers, NSA surveillance, executive privilege, executive lobbying, presidential reorganization authority, national security whistleblowing, covert spending, legislative vetoes, item vetoes, pocket vetoes, recess appointments, Congress and the Constitution, the Gramm-Rudman-Hollings Act, biennial budgeting, and the balanced budget amendment.

Fisher's specialties include constitutional law, national security law, budget policy, executive-legislative relations, and judicial-congressional relations. He is the author of more than four hundred articles in law reviews, political science journals, encyclopedias, books, magazines, and newspapers, and has been invited to speak in several dozen countries.